9780027944006

NEW YORK

By the staff of Editions Berlitz

Library of Congress Catalog Card Number:
78-52520

Printed in Switzerland by Weber S.A., Bienne.

**6th Printing
1984/1985 Edition**

How to use our guide

- All the practical information, hints and tips that you will need before and during the trip start on page 100, with a complete rundown of contents on page 103.

- For general background, see the sections New York and the New Yorkers, p. 6, and A Brief History, p. 12.

- All the sights to see are listed between pages 21 and 76. Our own choice of sights most highly recommended is pinpointed by the Berlitz traveller symbol.

- Entertainment, nightlife and all other leisure activities are described between pages 77 and 90, while information on restaurants and cuisine is to be found on pages 92 to 98.

- Finally, there is an index at the back of the book, pp. 126–128.

Although we make every effort to ensure the accuracy of all the information in this book, changes occur incessantly. We cannot therefore take responsibility for facts, prices, addresses and circumstances in general that are constantly subject to alteration. Our guides are updated on a regular basis as we reprint, and we are always grateful to readers who let us know of any errors, changes or serious omissions they come across.

Text: Martine Lamunière
Photography: Jean Mohr
Layout: Doris Haldemann
We're especially grateful to Kathy Mills and Ellen Stein for their help with the preparation of this guide.
Cartography: Falk-Verlag, Hamburg.

Contents

Maps

Photo, pp. 2–3: Central Park   5

New York and the New Yorkers

Okay, so New York is crowded, dirty, noisy and impolite! But it's one of the world's most exciting and beautiful cities and, surprisingly, a very human place.

Other Americans often fear and dislike New York. With a typical shrug, New Yorkers dismiss this as provincial jealousy. Fire sirens may wail all night while steam billows hellishly from the manholes, the subway cars may be defaced by graffiti, and people move faster than taxis. So what? New York is

the place where it's all happening!

This is the Big Apple: Wall Street and its dollars, Rockefeller Center with its multinational corporations, Madison Avenue manipulating the media, the United Nations with its diplomacy. Dynamic? And how!

Look at the nervous knot of pedestrians waiting for the traffic light to change: a Wall Street tycoon, pin-striped; a

Faces and races in the crowd: law-abiding New Yorkers cross with the traffic signal. At rush hour, walking can be faster than taking a taxi.

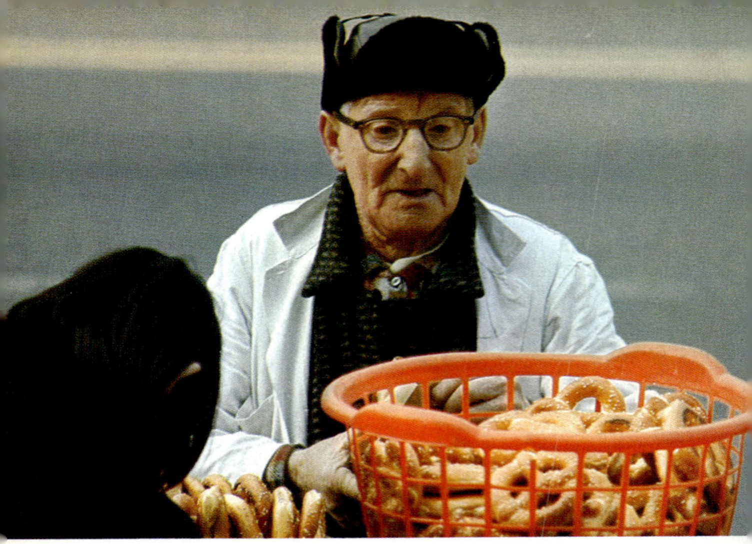

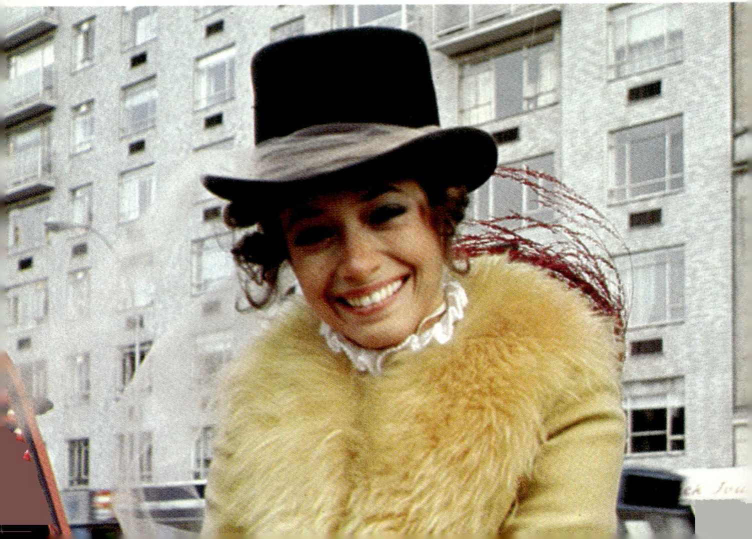

chic black model with her portfolio; an Orthodox Jew straight out of the Old Testament; a Latin American—more Latin than American but in a rush like everybody; to say nothing of the Chinese, Italians, Irish, Greeks, Eastern Europeans…

Even the language of New York—pronounced Noo Yawk —is not quite American. Spoken in a mumbled rush, it's a tough brand of English with the exaggeration of Madison Avenue, the sarcasm of the street-wise kid and a few words of Yiddish and Italian as punctuation.

New York is in many respects a "refugee camp", the largest in the world. The immigrants who didn't want to go any farther, who didn't want to be blended into the American melting pot, stayed here. They settled in New York to keep their own values and whatever they could preserve of their native culture. Variety and tolerance are the bywords in New York. You can do and say whatever you like—stand on your head in Columbus Circle or recite poetry in Wall Street —and nobody will look twice.

Pretzel-salesman and trendy girl are equally at home amidst varied cultures and values of New York.

Of course you'll want to see the skyscrapers. Chicago's may be more beautiful but those in Manhattan, the island heart of New York, will impress you with their overwhelming abundance. A veritable forest of glass and steel! Then, for a change of pace, explore some residential neighbourhoods. Greenwich Village will enchant you with its tree-lined streets (yes, real trees!) and tidy brownstone houses, reminiscent of London or Amsterdam. On the Upper West Side, you may smile at the huge Victorian apartment buildings topped with Moorish arches, Babylonian turrets or Gothic spires. In New York you need eyes in the top of your head.

First-time visitors are often nervous about New York because of its size, relentless pace and reputation for violence. Crime certainly is a problem, with roots in poverty. You don't have to venture far from the glittering centre to see desolate streets with abandoned and gutted buildings. New Yorkers don't try to hide the problem. They've simply had to learn to live with it.

Just relax and prepare for all the excitement of a great port, a fashion, financial, intellectual and cultural capital. Business and art coexist effortlessly here: **9**

New York in Figures

New York is bigger, taller and more impressive than anywhere else. If you want proof, here are a few figures:

– The five boroughs (Manhattan, Brooklyn, Queens, the Bronx and Staten Island) have a total population of 8 million. With the surrounding suburbs, this figure rises to 12 million, and if the outlying satellite cities are included, the total attains a phenomenal 16 million inhabitants.

– New York City covers an area of 300 square miles. It has 6,400 miles of streets and 18 miles of beaches. There are 1,100 parks, squares and playgrounds with a total area of 36,500 acres; 120 museums and 400 galleries; 30 department stores; 150 theatres; 3,500 churches, 28,000 restaurants, 100,000 first-class hotel rooms and 12,000 taxis.

– About 4 million people ride the subway every day. Some 2.5 million catch a bus. The number of shops is well up in the thousands. More than 16 million people visit New York each year, 2 million of them from overseas.

In New York there are more Italians than in Venice, more Irish than in Dublin and more Jews than in any other city in the world.

a museum guide will proudly tell you how much a Rembrandt cost. From a pharaoh's tomb to pop art, New York money has endowed dozens of memorable museums. It's the creative-arts centre of the U.S.A., perhaps the world. Broadway invented the musical and crowds queue up

in Central Park to see free Shakespeare. You could easily while away an afternoon immersed in the *Sunday Times'* section on current ballet, opera and concert performances.

But do save some time for shopping, too. From discount emporia to that esoteric item you've always been looking for, not to mention the enormous choice in everything. And don't miss this unique opportunity for a whirlwind gastronomic tour of the globe. Whether

Balancing act—giant Noguchi cube animates environment.

charcoal broiled or whipped up in a *wok*, you name it, New York's got it!

Yes, everything about New York is excessive, including the climate: too hot in summer, too cold in winter. "You have to be a little crazy to live in New York", according to a subway poster, "crazy about shows, restaurants, theatres, shopping". New Yorkers, with their well-concealed hearts of gold, really do love their town. They hope you will, too.

A Brief History

When Giovanni da Verrazzano, a Florentine in the service of France, set foot on Staten Island, he hardly dreamed that the bay he had discovered would one day become the site of the most powerful city in the world. That was in 1524, just 32 years after Christopher Columbus's first voyage to America. Today a bridge bearing his name (but spelled with one "z") stretches across New York Bay.

NEW YORK CITY

Verrazzano was well received by the Manhattans, a local tribe of Indians who guided his ship to a safe landing. Though he wrote an enthusiastic report of his visit to the French king, Francis I, a century passed before any settlers came to live on the estuary. This was the period of discovery and the major European countries were preoccupied with exploration and staking claims, not with establishing colonies.

New Amsterdam
In 1609 the East India Company of Holland sent an Englishman, Henry Hudson, to look for a westward route to the Indies. He didn't find what he was after but he sailed up the broad river (later named after him) that empties into the bay and discovered the beautiful, bountiful Hudson Valley. Returning to Holland with quantities of furs, fruit and tobacco, Hudson stirred up a good deal of interest. A group of merchants founded the United New Netherland Company, which was to have a trading monopoly in the area. Then, in 1621, the Dutch West India Company was granted the charter to trade, plant colonies and defend their outposts in North and South America. The first settlers arrived under their auspices in 1624, ousting the French who were there only hours before them. The following spring, they built a small town on the southern end of Manhattan Island and called it New Amsterdam.

For 40 years the Dutch remained in possession of Manhattan, purchased from the Indians for the legendary sum of $24. Under the leadership of two governors, Peter Minuit and Peter Stuyvesant, the town took on a Dutch look, yet from the beginning it was the most cosmopolitan centre in the New World. The earliest immigrants included Walloons, Scandinavians, Germans, Englishmen, Spaniards, and Portuguese Jews, not to mention black slaves from the Caribbean. In 1643 a priest counted 18 languages spoken in this town of 1,500 inhabitants. Other settlements had developed outside of Manhattan in what is now the Bronx (founded by Jonas Bronck, a Dane), in the Flushing area of Queens and in Brooklyn.

Life was by no means easy, though. In those days of poor communications, it was practically impossible to do anything without prior approval from the home country. Relations **13** with the Indians were tense and the climate was harsh. What's more, the British—who held all the colonies around New York—were knocking at the door.

Unable or unwilling to put up a fight, the Dutch settlers surrendered to the Duke of York's troops on September 8, 1664. New Amsterdam was rechristened New York. At first, things changed very little. The Dutch briefly retook the city in 1673 (renaming it New Orange), but by the Treaty of Westminster of the following year, Manhattan and New Netherland became definitively English. Ceding to popular pressure, the British governor allowed the election in 1683 of a provincial assembly, which divided the colony into 12 counties. Kings County was named in honour of Charles II of England, Queens for his wife and Richmond for his son.

In the 18th century, the town grew into a city of 25,000. Life became more pleasant. A city hall and several fine churches were built and King's College and the city's first newspaper established. Many traders were able to make their fortunes. However, the people were increasingly irked by British control. New York, like the other colonies, was split between "loyalists" to the Crown and "patriots" who favoured independence. On June 27, 1775, half the town went to cheer Washington as he left to take command of the Revolutionary Army in Boston, while the other half was down at the harbour giving a rousing welcome to the English governor, who had just returned from London. Similarly, the New York delegates voted against an early version of the Declaration of Independence. But a few days later, when the final text had been drafted, they signed it. Even in those days New Yorkers were a people apart from other Americans.

The New Republic
After a series of battles around New York, their last stronghold, the English finally gave up in 1783, recognizing the independence of the American colonies. Washington returned triumphantly to New York and bade farewell to his troops at Fraunces Tavern (see p. 42). He came back again on another auspicious occasion: to take the oath of office as the first president of the new United States on the balcony of Federal Hall. At that time, New York was the national capital.

In the early 19th century, New York was much richer culturally than any other American city. The political capital had moved to Philadelphia in 1790 but New York developed as the country's shipping and commercial centre. In 1800, the population was 60,000—twice what it had been ten years earlier. Already the city had problems that persist today: housing shortages, too few policemen and firemen, not enough water and inadequate public transportation facilities. Epidemics were frequent, sometimes forcing people to "escape" to Greenwich Village for the summer.

In 1811 the legislature decided that further growth of New York must be regulated. A special commission submitted a revolutionary plan: all new streets should henceforth cross each other at right angles with avenues running north-south and streets east-west. The plan was immediately adopted, heralding the birth of Manhattan as we know it today.

Burgeoning Town

When the Erie Canal opened in 1825, New York became the ocean gateway for the Great Lakes region. Business flourished and shipyards abounded in this major port, but even so there was too little work for newcomers. Blacks, Irish and Germans lived on top of each other in crowded shanty towns. The Catholic Irish were resented, and religious conflicts erupted. It was at this time that the American press began to play a highly influential role in politics. Hotly debated issues of the day included state support for Catholic schools, the immigrants' right to vote and the abolition of slavery.

In December 1835, a terrible fire destroyed the heart of the business district, including all that remained from the Dutch era. But the city recovered with amazing speed. Old neighbourhoods were soon rebuilt with the new, wealthy banks putting up the buildings that still stand in Wall Street. There was much new construction uptown, too: in 1853, the Crystal Palace of the first American World's Fair went up, and five years later work started on Central Park and St. Patrick's Cathedral. In spite of the new prosperity, this was also a very turbulent period for New York. Between 1840 and 1860 the city's population rose from 300,000 to 800,000. Riots, demonstrations and street fights were not uncommon.

With the Civil War, the town's growth came to a temporary halt. New Yorkers were markedly unenthusiastic about **15**

Ghosts of millions of immigrants haunt deserted quarantine station, Ellis Island in New York harbour.

the Union cause, and the draft law—providing for a $300 exemption fee—met with ferocious opposition from the foreign-born working class. In July 1863, three days of rioting resulted in upwards of 500 deaths.

After the war, the boom continued unabated to the end of the century. It gave rise to unprecedented corruption on a vast scale and to wild property speculation. Financiers Jay Gould and Jim Fisk cornered the gold market, ruining half of Wall Street on "Black Friday" in September 1869. Boss Tweed of the Tammany Hall political organization ran New York with his cohorts and managed to fleece the city of something like $200 million. Many great fortunes were made more or less honestly. The Vanderbilts constructed the railroads, and the Morgans, the banking tycoons, amassed fabulous art collections in an effort to gain acceptance among the "old families." This same period saw the foundation of the Metropolitan Museum, the Natural History Museum and the public libraries.

16

Mass Immigration

During the second half of the century, immigrants flooded in to New York in search of a new life. They came from Ireland and Germany as always but now also from Italy, Russia, Poland and Hungary. The first major wave of Jewish settlers arrived in the eighties. Over 2 million newcomers landed in New York between 1885 and 1895, welcomed (after 1886) by the newly inaugurated Statue of Liberty (see p. 70). For the

first time Congress imposed limits on immigration, banning Chinese, sick people, madmen and anarchists.

Adequate housing for the constantly expanding working population was a great problem. A subsidized housing programme was launched but could hardly begin to deal with the situation. The new middle class moved to West Side neighbourhoods near Central Park, and the "El" or elevated train was built to serve these districts. In 1870 construction started on a bridge to connect New York and Brooklyn, by then a town in its own right. The invention of the elevator made it possible to put up "skyscrapers" eight or ten stories high. There was a new vogue for department stores. Alexander Graham Bell demonstrated his telephone in New York in May of 1877. By October there were already 252 subscribers and the first New York telephone directory ap-

ALL THINGS
BRIGHT & BEAUTIFUL
ANTIQUES
PILLOWS GIFTS QUILTS
13
Saint
Marks
Place

peared. Electric lights were installed in many new buildings.

In 1898 New York (henceforth known as Manhattan), Brooklyn, Queens, the Bronx and Staten Island amalgamated into Greater New York with a population of over 3 million. The early years of this century saw the first genuine skyscrapers: the Flatiron building (1902) reached a height of 286 feet with 21 floors. In 1904, the first subway line opened. Greenwich Village, which became a centre for artists, writers and theatre people, acquired a reputation for bohemianism. Following World War I, the exclusive shops and more fashionable department stores moved to Fifth Avenue above 34th Street and New York had to cope with traffic jams.

In the twenties, theatre, baseball and jazz all drew large crowds. Aviator Charles Lindbergh received a memorable hero's welcome in 1927 after his solo flight across the Atlantic. About 300 tons of confetti fluttered down on the streets of New York.

In October 1929 the business boom screeched to a sudden halt with the crash of the stock market. Breadlines and apple sellers became a common sight, and a shantytown sprang up in Central Park. In 1934, a dynamic mayor by the name of Fiorello La Guardia fought for public welfare measures and civic reform. He rebuilt much of the Lower East Side, but, unfortunately, Harlem remained, becoming the home not only of the blacks but also of the Puerto Ricans who arrived in the last wave of immigration.

World City

When the United Nations decided to set up their headquarters in New York after the Second World War, the town started calling itself "World City." It is an apt title. Throughout the 350 years of its history, New York has been the most cosmopolitan of cities. In 1970, almost 19 per cent of its 8 million inhabitants had been born abroad. Nine foreign-language dailies are still published here as each little community tries to retain its individuality.

In recent years, the city has often seemed to be on the brink of disaster. Financial problems have threatened to topple the mighty metropolis. New York, which had always been first and foremost, has had to take stock. But it's certainly premature to proclaim the demise of this city that has been a symbol of opportunity for so long.

What to See

The real New York, of course, includes more than Manhattan. The boroughs of Brooklyn, Queens, Staten Island and the Bronx are important elements in the city's life. But the average tourist with a limited amount of time for sightseeing wants to hit the highlights. And there's no denying that Manhattan—the island queen of the metropolis, $13\frac{1}{2}$ miles long and 2 miles wide—is where he'll find them.

Midtown

Most hotels are located in midtown, right in the centre of Manhattan. If this is where you're staying, then you'll have no difficulty in getting around the immediate area on foot.

Rockefeller Center

Symbol of the power and wealth of New York, this massive group of buildings—21 in all—stretches from 48th to 53rd Street between Fifth Avenue and the Avenue of the Americas (still generally known as Sixth Avenue). Decisions taken here today in this communications hub are likely to figure in tomorrow's papers.

When Columbia University acquired the site in 1811 it consisted of farmlands and a botanical garden. Towards the end of the century the district became quite fashionable and handsome private homes were built. Then during Prohibition speakeasies (clandestine bars) moved in and the middle class moved out. Columbia had trouble finding tenants. In 1928 John D. Rockefeller asked the university for a lease on the 17-acre site, renewable until 2069. He had all the buildings demolished to make way for a vast business centre. The first skyscrapers, linked by a network of underground galleries filled with shops and restaurants, were finished by the early thirties.

From Fifth Avenue you enter by the **Channel Promenade,** a pedestrian alley with handsome fountains and floral displays. On the left you'll find the Maison Française, on the right the British Empire Building. At the end is the ice-skating rink, in summer a garden terrace. Behind it hovers the massive bronze figure of Prometheus and in winter a Christmas tree, billed as the world's tallest. The massive RCA Building looms over it all. Take the elevator to the 65th floor to purchase a ticket for the **Observation Roof** on the 69th floor. The view of Manhattan is magnificent. **21**

The Rainbow Room is on the 65th floor. The view from this supper club is just as fabulous. You can eat there or just sit at the bar for a cocktail: the price of a drink is not exorbitant.

Several floors of the RCA Building are occupied by NBC, the radio and television network.

Guided tours of Rockefeller Center include the Observation Roof and a visit to the famous

Prometheus statue presides over Rockefeller Center café tables.

Finding Your Way Around

It is virtually impossible to get lost on Manhattan: no other town in the world is built on such simple lines. The backbone of the island is Fifth Avenue; all areas to the west of it as far as the Hudson are known as the "West Side", while the "East Side" covers

the area between Fifth Avenue and the East River. Fifth Avenue begins at Washington Square in Greenwich Village.

"West 53rd Street" is the address of a building on 53rd Street, just west of Fifth Avenue. One will often hear people say "That's three blocks away". (A block is a group of buildings surrounded on four sides by streets and/or avenues.) And it's quite common to give an address as the point where two roads meet: "60th and Lexington".

Apart from the Wall Street area and Greenwich Village, where the streets have names and still follow the lines laid down in colonial days, all roads intersect at right-angles and all streets are numbered. Avenues (First to Twelfth) run north-south, streets (1st to 220th) run east-west. Some of the avenues also have names, such as Lexington, Madison, Park and Avenue of the Americas (often called Sixth Avenue). Broadway is the only one that doesn't follow a straight line.

Downtown means Manhattan south of 34th Street. Midtown speaks for itself. Uptown is the area north of 59th Street.

Americans refer to the ground floor as the first, and few buildings, believe it or not, have a 13th floor.

23

MIDTOWN MANHATTAN

Franklin D. Roosevelt Drive

York Ave.

First Ave.

Second Ave.

Third Ave.

Lexington Ave.

Park Ave.

Madison Ave.

Fifth Ave.

York Ave.

First Ave.

Second Ave.

Third Ave.

Lexington Ave.

Park Ave.

Madison Ave.

Fifth Ave.

E. 90th St.
E. 86th St.
E. 81st St.
E. 79th St.
E. 74th St.
E. 72nd St.
E. 70th St.
E. 65th St.

N.Y. Hospital

Memorial Hospital

Rockefeller University of Medical Research

YORKVILLE

EAST SIDE

Hunter College

Metropolitan Museum of Art

Whitney Museum of American Art

Frick Collection

Museum of the City of New York, Jewish Museum

Guggenheim Museum

Reservoir

Central Park

Cleopatra's Needle

Delacorte Theatre

The Lake

Bethesda Fountain

The Mall

The Sheep Meadow

Tavern on the Green

Zoo

Arsenal

Wollman Memorial Rink

Central Park West

Central Park West

W. 65th St.

Columbus Ave.

Columbus Ave.

Amsterdam Ave.

Amsterdam

West End Ave.

West End Ave.

W. 86th St.
W. 90th St.
W. 81st St.
W. 79th St.
W. 74th St.
W. 72nd St.
W. 70th St.

American Museum of Natural History

N.Y. Historical Society

WEST SIDE

Columbia University, The Cloisters

Broadway

Juilliard School

Philharmonic Hall

N.Y. State Theater

Vivian Beaumont Theater

Metropolitan Opera House

LINCOLN CENTER

Riverside Drive

Riverside Park

Henry Hudson Parkway

Riverside Drive

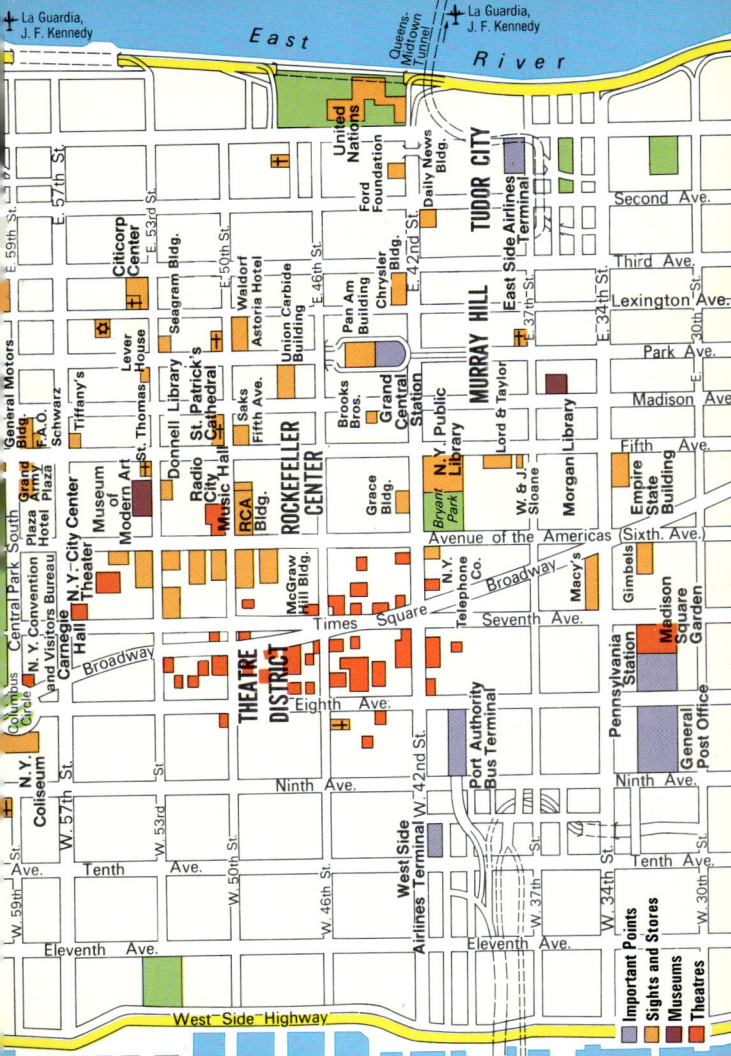

La Guardia, J. F. Kennedy

La Guardia, J. F. Kennedy

East River

Queens-Midtown Tunnel

United Nations

Daily News Bldg.

TUDOR CITY

East Side Airlines Terminal

Second Ave.

Ford Foundation

Chrysler Bldg.

Third Ave.

Citicorp Center

Seagram Bldg.

Waldorf Astoria Hotel

Union Carbide Building

Pan Am Building

MURRAY HILL

Lexington Ave.

E. 57th St.
E. 59th St.
E. 53rd St.
E. 50th St.
E. 46th St.
E. 42nd St.
E. 37th St.
E. 34th St.
E. 30th St.

General Motors Bldg.

Lever House

St. Thomas Church

St. Patrick's Cathedral

Saks Fifth Ave.

Brooks Bros.

Grand Central Station

Park Ave.

Madison Ave.

F.A.O. Schwarz

Tiffany's

Donnell Library

Radio City Music Hall

N.Y. Public Library

Lord & Taylor

Morgan Library

Fifth Ave.

Grand Army Plaza

Museum of Modern Art

RCA Bldg.

ROCKEFELLER CENTER

Grace Bldg.

Bryant Park

W. & J. Sloane

Empire State Building

Central Park South

N.Y. Convention and Visitors Bureau

Plaza Hotel

N.Y. City Center Theater

McGraw Hill Bldg.

Avenue of the Americas (Sixth Ave.)

N.Y. Telephone Co.

Broadway

Macy's

Gimbels

Madison Square Garden

Carnegie Hall

Times Square

Seventh Ave.

Columbus Circle

Broadway

THEATRE DISTRICT

Eighth Ave.

Port Authority Bus Terminal

Pennsylvania Station

General Post Office

N.Y. Coliseum

Ninth Ave.

Ninth Ave.

W. 57th St.
W. 53rd St.
W. 50th St.
W. 46th St.
W. 42nd St.
W. 37th St.
W. 34th St.
W. 30th St.

West Side Airlines Terminal

W. 59th Ave.

Tenth Ave.

Tenth Ave.

Eleventh Ave.

Eleventh Ave.

West Side Highway

Important Points
Sights and Stores
Museums
Theatres

Radio City Music Hall. They leave from the Guided Tour Office on the main floor of the RCA Building near the 50th-Street entrance. For hours, see p. 120.

Radio City Music Hall, also on the east side of Avenue of the Americas, is the largest indoor movie theatre in the world with a seating capacity of over 6,000. A symbol of the period when everything Americans did had to be better and above all bigger, Radio City holds all the records: the largest Wurlitzer organ in the world, the biggest chandeliers, a revolving stage on three levels, plus lounges downstairs decorated in 1930s Hollywood style.

If you have a spare evening, be sure to take in one of the shows. You'll be able to hear the famous organ and Radio City's own symphony orchestra. Special shows feature the Rockettes, since 1926 America's most famous troupe of dancing girls, kicking up their legs in perfect time.

The Music Hall was scheduled to close in 1979, but Radio City lovers joined forces to save this nostalgic monument.

Emerging from Radio City, you have a marvellous view of the most attractive ensemble of modern **skyscrapers** in New York. To the south on the west side of Sixth Avenue, stands the McGraw-Hill Building (see p. 70), then the Exxon Building, next Time-Life, Equitable Life, J.C. Penney, the Hilton Hotel and finally Burlington House.

Fifth Avenue

Fifth Avenue suggests luxury not just in the States but all over the world. It used to be the home of millionaires who lived between 34th and 50th streets until around 1900, when they started moving to Central Park, making way for fancy stores. The most exclusive are to be found between 47th Street (centre of the diamond merchants, well worth a detour) and Central Park South, barely a dozen blocks: Saks Fifth Avenue, Henri Bendel, Bergdorf Goodman, the luxury department stores; Cartier, Tiffany, Van Cleef & Arpels, the jewellers; boutiques of the French and Italian couturiers; the famous leather goods stores; and a number of excellent bookshops. Between 50th and 51st streets is **St. Patrick's Cathedral,** a more or less exact copy of Cologne's Gothic cathedral.

The **Grand Army Plaza,** in the corner of Central Park

South, marks the division between the shopping area of Fifth Avenue and the residential section, lined with mansions and de luxe apartment buildings. You'll pass by here on your way to one of the nearby museums. This is the place to hire a horse-drawn carriage for a ride around Central Park (see p. 56). (see p. 56) It's also the site of two of New York's smartest hotels, the Plaza and the Pierre (at 61st). Across from the Plaza, set a little way back from the avenue, is a modern skyscraper designed by Edward Stone, the General Motors headquarters.

Take a look, too, at the succession of **skyscrapers**

along Madison Avenue—especially AT&T's controversial post-modernist pile at 56th Street, the work of the Johnson-Burgee firm, and the IBM building (57th) by Edward Larabee Barnes, which links up to Trump Tower in Fifth Avenue. The 57-storey tower of the Helmsley Palace Hotel (Madison between 50th and 51st) incorporates the Neo-Renaissance Villard Houses, a New York landmark since 1885.

Times Square and Broadway

Times Square, on the north side of 42nd Street between Broadway and Seventh Avenue, got its name from the *New York Times* which set up its offices here in 1904. But Times Square, of course, refers to more than just one square; it covers the area from 42nd to 47th Streets, between Sixth and Eighth avenues. The best theatres and first-run cinemas are to be found here, but so are strip joints (or worse), pornographic bookstores and films and prostitutes. Here you find excellent restaurants alongside seamy

Sordid or glamorous, Times Square remains liveliest entertainment area.

bars; at night you'll see women in evening dress arriving in chauffeur-driven Rolls, as well as tramps, drunks, pickpockets, drug-pushers and sundry street musicians. Times Square seems pretty sordid by day, but in the evenings when the neon lights glow and the litter is not as noticeable, it comes alive.

The famous moving illuminated news tape at No. 1 Times Square is made up of more than 12,000 electric bulbs. On December 31, a lighted globe comes down a pole on the top of this building announcing the arrival of the New Year. Tens of thousands of New Yorkers come to witness this event, which is also shown on television.

In some ways **Broadway** and Times Square overlap. A legitimate theatre will be described as "on Broadway" whereas a pornographic cinema at the very same address would be "in Times Square". Practically all popular plays and musical comedies are produced "on Broadway." The term has become such a cliché that a serious theatre will advertise itself as "off-Broadway", while the real avant-garde will claim to be "off-off Broadway". This has nothing to do with geographical location. (See also p. 83.)

42nd Street

West of Times Square, 42nd Street is known as "Sin Street". You'll understand why when you see it. But going east, on the other hand, it's one of the liveliest, most fascinating streets in the city. This has always been the place for pace-setting buildings: here you'll see some of the greatest successes in the history of American architecture.

At 42nd Street and Sixth Avenue are two of the most attractive skyscrapers of recent years (both completed in 1974): the **New York Telephone Company Building** on the corner—all white marble and black glass—and the **W.R. Grace Building** between Fifth and Sixth avenues, with its striking, slightly concave silhouette. The same architect, Gordon Bunshaft, designed an almost identical building on 57th Street, a few steps from Fifth Avenue. They're both magnificent.

Bryant Park occupies the site of the Crystal Palace, built for the 1853 World's Fair and destroyed by fire six years later. The park, not recommended after dark, lies behind the **New York Public Library.** This mo-

Benevolent Uncle Sam advertises charity drive outside main library.

nument in American Beaux-Arts style (neo-classic) opened in 1911; two well-photographed stone lions guard the entrance. One of the largest libraries in the world, it possesses several million books, almost as many manuscripts and vast reading rooms. A number of rare works are put on exhibit in rotation. Unfortunately, this cultural monument is under constant threat of bankruptcy. Entrance is free. Closed on Thursday, Sunday and holidays.

Further east on 42nd Street, past Madison Avenue, you will come to the Airline Building, a minor masterpiece of Art Deco which was an air terminal before World War II. Almost across the street, blocking the view up Park Avenue is the massive bulk of **Grand Central Station,** completed in 1913. Inside 66 rail lines arrive on the upper level, 57 on the lower. The central concourse, one of the largest in the world, is invaded every afternoon from 4 to 5.30 by hundreds of thousands of suburban commuters catching their trains home. New Yorkers either love or hate the place, and attempts have been made more than once to have it torn down. It is now classified as a national monument, an example of American Beaux-Arts style.

A network of passageways links Grand Central to nearby hotels, office buildings and the subway. They're lined with all kinds of shops and several restaurants, including the venerable Oyster Bar, a New York institution.

Directly behind the station is the **Pan Am Building,** the head office of the airline, where more than 20,000 people work. Cutting across Park Avenue, the 59-floor octagonal structure is

easily recognized even from afar. Escalators lead directly into Grand Central Station. As a result of an accident in 1977, helicopters are now banned from using the rooftop heliport.

Don't miss four New York landmarks on Park Avenue north of the Pan Am Building: on the left, at 47th Street, the striking **Union Carbide Building** with its pink marble pavement; at 49th Street the **Waldorf Astoria Hotel** (on the right), distinguished host to visiting heads of state; the beautiful bronze **Seagram Building,** by Mies van der Rohe and Philip Johnson, rises on the right between 52nd and 53rd streets; and, across the avenue at 53rd Street, the **Lever House,**

Epidemic of graffiti on subway train has evolved into a new art form.

a green glass structure which created an architectural furor when it was built in 1952.

Back on 42nd Street you'll come to the **Chrysler Building.** When completed in 1930, this was the tallest skyscraper in the world, but in a matter of months it was overtaken by the Empire State Building. Chrysler is a positive temple to the automobile: the top is shaped like the radiator cap on Chrysler's 1929 model and the whole façade is dotted with stylized automobile motifs. Although architecturally one of the most original efforts in New York, it is now just another office building.

At the corner of Second Avenue stands the Daily News Building, the home of the newspaper with the largest daily circulation in America. An enormous revolving globe occupies a good part of the lobby.

Further on, between Second and First Avenues, you will pass the offices of the Ford Foundation with a marvellous interior garden you can see from the street.

Then you arrive at U.N. Plaza.

In the concrete world of Manhattan nature is never far away.

The United Nations

It was John D. Rockefeller, Jr., who donated the 18-acre site in order to persuade the members of the U.N. to set up their headquarters in New York. A team of 11 architects including American Wallace K. Harrison, Swiss Le Corbusier and Brazilian Oscar Niemeyer designed the buildings, completed in the early 1950s. The Secretariat is housed in the tower, and the General Assembly meets in the lower block with the slightly concave roof. The complex includes two other buildings: the Dag Hammarskjöld Library, a memorial to the former secretary general, and the Conference Building. The U.N. complex is more spectacular from the river (or Queens) than from First Avenue.

Only a few rooms in the Secretariat are open to the public, but when the General Assembly is in session, visitors can usually attend meetings. Entrance is free, but you must obtain a ticket from the information desk in the lobby (45th Street and First Avenue). This is also the starting point for **guided tours** (times are listed under SIGHTSEEING HOURS, pp. 119–121). The tour, which lasts an hour, takes you behind the scenes and explains how the **35**

U.N. works. Most member states have donated works of art which are on display in the Conference Building. These include Persian rugs, North African mosaics, a Chagall stained glass panel, among other treasures. The Security Council Room was a gift from Norway, the Trusteeship Council Room from Denmark and the Economic and Social Council Room from Sweden.

You can buy a sandwich to eat in the garden while you admire the strikingly beautiful skyscrapers lining U.N. Plaza, or you can eat in the Delegates' Dining Room, which overlooks the East River, before noon or after 2 p.m. It's advisable to reserve your table at the information desk in the lobby. There is a coffee-shop in the central hall on the lower level. A shop specializing in crafts from all over the world is the place to find original gifts at very reasonable prices. The bookshop sells U.N. publications, and if you are a stamp collector you shouldn't miss the post office which sells U.N. stamps valid only if posted within the complex.

U.N. complex dominates East River waterfront; tallest spire on skyline is Chrysler building, built in 1930.

Empire State Building

On the corner of Fifth Avenue and 34th Street, the Empire State Building is open to the public every day from 9.30 a.m. until midnight. It is no longer the tallest building in the world, and Americans tend to overrate it when they call it "the cathedral of the skies" or "the eighth wonder of the world". But it's something you shouldn't miss

King Kong is fondly remembered in Empire State Building souvenir shop.

—unless of course it's a foggy day. Everything about the Empire State Building is huge: 102 stories; 60,000 tons of steel; 3,500 miles of telephone wires and cables; 60 miles of pipes; a volume of $1\frac{1}{4}$ million cubic yards; 1,860 steps and, last but not least, a height of 1,472 feet!

To reach the Observation Deck you first have to go down to the basement level (don't worry about getting lost, there are plenty of arrows to guide you). There you buy your ticket and get in line. Or if it interests you, look in on the Guinness World Records Exhibit, next to the ticket office. The items on display include a hair split 14 times, the longest earthworm in the world, the biggest guitar, the smallest violin, the thinnest waist, the longest beard and many other similar world record holders.

An elevator will speed you up to the 80th floor in less than a minute. You'll just have time to catch your breath and get your ears unblocked before taking a second elevator to the 86th floor, 1,050 feet above street level. In winter you can stay inside the heated shelter of the observatory. In summer enjoy the **view** from the outside terrace. On a clear day you can make out the funnels of ships 40 miles out at sea. The view is really superb day or night.

If you're not discouraged by the line of people, you can take a third elevator right up to the open roof on the 102nd floor. There you will be at the foot of the largest antenna in the world (222 feet high and weighing 70 tons), a relay station for all the television channels in the metropolitan region.

When you emerge from the Empire State Building, turn west along 34th Street, where you'll find some of the most popular department stores. A visit to Macy's is a must (see p. 81). Nearby, at Seventh Avenue and 31st Street, is **Madison Square Garden,** renowned for boxing matches and various entertainment attractions including the circus, home of the New York "Knicks" (basketball) and the Rangers (hockey), but also used as a conference centre. The Garden seats 20,000 and the Felt Forum holds an additional 5,000.

Below Madison Square Garden is **Pennsylvania Station** (invariably referred to as Penn Station), the railway terminal for Long Island and New Jersey commuters and for many of the fast, long-distance trains.

Next to Madison Square Garden, at Eighth Avenue and 33rd Street, you'll find New York's General Post Office. **39**

Downtown

Wall Street Area

Wall Street, located at the southern tip of Manhattan, is the financial district and, in some respects, the most impressive part of New York. Here you really feel you're at the very heart of the world's greatest power. The skyscrapers, closer together than elsewhere, look all the more massive, and the streets are veritable canyons.

Wall Street itself got its name from the stockade (really a wall of boards) built here in 1653 by the Dutch governor Peter Stuyvesant to protect New Amsterdam from the Indians. It didn't do much good because the settlers persisted in carting off planks for their own uses. Today Wall Street is the home of all the big banks in the world of finance. No address anywhere holds greater prestige. Among those with head offices here are Chase Manhattan and Morgan Guaranty Trust.

On the corner of Wall and Nassau streets is the **Federal Hall National Memorial.** The original building, demolished in 1812, was for a year the home of the United States Congress. On April 30, 1789, George Washington took the oath as the first president of the United States here. The Hall's hours are listed on p. 120.

The **New York Stock Exchange,** across the way, is the largest in the United States and well worth a visit. The entrance at 20 Broad Street leads into the visitors' gallery, open during most of the Exchange's trading hours (see p. 120). From there, you'll have a bird's-eye view of the trading floor. You may not have the slightest idea of what's going on, but the sight is one you'll never forget. You can learn about the workings of the Exchange from a permanent exhibit and a film, as well as a guided tour. A demonstration of the famous ticker tape is also featured.

After the stress and strain of the stock market, relax for a bit in one of the coolest spots in Manhattan—**Battery Park** on the southern tip of the island. You have a splendid view of New York Bay. The round fortress on the water is **Castle Clinton.** Built in 1811 but never used for military purposes, it was later converted to a theatre and renamed Castle Garden. Lafayette was received here with great ceremony in 1825. From 1855 to 1890 Castle Garden served as an immigration reception centre: 7 million Europeans passed through this **41**

building. Until 1941 it housed an aquarium. Now classified as a historical monument, Castle Clinton has been restored to its original state and name and contains a small museum.

On the corner of Pearl and Broad streets stands **Fraunces Tavern,** built as a home in 1719 then converted to a tavern in 1763 by Samuel Fraunces. It was here in the Long Room that George Washington bid his officers farewell after the Revolutionary War on December 4, 1783. Now owned by the Sons of the Revolution in the State of New York, it houses the Fraunces Tavern Museum, which features permanent and changing exhibits on the Revolutionary War and 18th-century American history and culture, an audiovisual presentation on the early history of New York City, and a regular programme of lectures and concerts. On the ground floor is the Fraunces Tavern Restaurant.

Returning to Nassau Street, behind Federal Hall you can admire the shining glass and aluminum tower of the **Chase Manhattan Bank,** built in 1961. About 15,000 people work in

Wall Street's unlikely neighbours: hubbub of Stock Exchange, calm of Trinity Church's old cemetery.

this 65-storey structure. The plaza leading to the building contains some very good modern statues by Japanese sculptor Isamu Noguchi and Frenchman Jean Dubuffet.

The Episcopalian **Trinity Church** on Broadway and Wall Street was built in 1846 in neo-Gothic style with bronze doors copied from the Baptistery in Florence. Some 280 feet high, the spire holds a bell dating from the 18th century. In the adjacent cemetery you can see the tombstones of many illustrious Americans, including Alexander Hamilton, one of the Founding Fathers, Robert Fulton, inventor of the

steamboat, and Albert Gallatin, Secretary of the Treasury under Thomas Jefferson. Trinity Church is one of New York's richest landlords, with extensive holdings going back to colonial times

A little further uptown, between Broadway and Park Row, you'll find the **City Hall,** built between 1803 and 1812. The offices of the mayor of New York are located here. There's also an interesting collection of portraits and furniture from the federal period. See p. 119 for opening hours.

You need no directions to find the twin towers of the **World Trade Center:** they're visible all over town. Not (quite) the tallest buildings in the world, the figures are nonetheless impressive: 1,350 feet high with 43,600 windows. Each tower has 23 express and 72 local elevators, as well as 4 for freight. The whole centre covers an area of 16 acres. It is served by various subway lines, including the PATH system to New Jersey, which disgorges tens of thousands of commuters every morning. The stations are accessible from the concourse (street) level, the site of a vast shopping centre, open Monday through Saturday, and numerous restaurants.

Even if your time in New York is limited, try to fit in a visit to the top of the World Trade Center. The observation deck on the 107th floor of Two World Trade Center dominates the city. And, weather permitting, you can go even higher— to the open-air rooftop promenade above the 110th floor, the highest outdoor observation platform in the world. The famous restaurant Windows on the World is located on the 107th floor of One World Trade Center.

The Port Authority of New York and New Jersey was responsible for building the Center, inaugurated in 1970. Besides the two 110-storey towers with their thousands of offices, there are four lower buildings in the complex, including a 22-storey hotel. A gigantic bronze fountain globe highlights the central square.

The 30 million cubic feet of earth and rocks excavated from the site were dumped into the Hudson River adjacent to the Trade Center, forming a great esplanade where an office complex and luxury apartment houses are being built.

The completion of the World Trade Center has brought new life to downtown New York. Not long ago, the area was vir-

44

tually deserted in the evening and at weekends. But the picture is changing rapidly as the residential population grows and the World Trade Center hotel and restaurants attract a weekend clientele.

Redevelopment has changed the face of **South Street Seaport,** a historic enclave on the East River, just south-west of Brooklyn Bridge. The Fulton Fish Market, a New York landmark for 100 years, has

Fritz Koenig's 25-foot-high globe in the World Trade Center Plaza.

been renovated to accommodate both the old-time fish wholesalers and a trendy new profusion of small food shops and restaurants. More shops and restaurants occupy premises in the refurbished red brick warehouses of Schermerhorn Row, dating from the early 1800s. Museum Block, an ensemble of buildings across from the fish market, incorporates gallery and theatre space, while the sailing ships tied up at piers 15 and 16 are now museums, too, open to visitors.

Lower East Side

At the turn of the century, the period of the main waves of immigration, many newcomers moved into the Lower East Side. The vast majority of them stayed only a few years, long enough to learn English, find a job and set off to make a living elsewhere in the United States. Some stayed on, though, and today three small ethnic enclaves remain on the Lower East Side: Chinatown, Little Italy and the Jewish quarter.

Tourists should be careful and discreet when visiting the Lower East Side. In any case, visits after nightfall are unadvisable.

If you take the subway to **46 Chinatown,** you won't go wrong: the Canal Street Station has signs in both Roman and Chinese characters. The telephone booths have pagoda roofs, narrow shops sell ivory and jade jewellery, grocers display Chinese cabbage, winter melon and snow peas and countless restaurants tumble over one another with their Cantonese, Shanghai and Szechwan specialities.

Some 10,000 Chinese live in the area between Canal Street, the Bowery, Park Row, Pearl Street and Center Street—some nine square blocks. For many years the Chinese were one of the most oppressed minorities in the United States. Immigration began at the time of the California gold rush. The Chinese, who came like everyone else to make their fortunes, quickly realized that there was not enough gold to go around, so they signed on as ranch and railroad workers.

You will see some very poor Chinese in Chinatown. They have integrated very little; many of them barely understand English and still speak Chinese to their children. They read only Chinese newspapers

New York's Chinatown keeps out "foreign" influences, except for barber's familiar striped pole.

and are more concerned about events in Peking than in Washington. (Many went into mourning when Mao-Tse-Tung died.)

If you can, go there on the weekend, when all the Chinese of the New York area turn up to do their weekly shopping. Do go into one of the supermarkets on Canal Street. They sell the best tea in the world and very pretty porcelain at rock-bottom prices; you'll see wonderful hanging ducks and hundreds of mysterious delicacies. You can take a look at the Chinese Museum (8 Mott Street) and the Buddhist Temple (64 Mott Street). Don't miss the Chinese New Year Festival (see p. 87).

Leave Chinatown by way of Chatham Square and St. James Place. You will come almost immediately to the Jewish cemetery, Shearith Israel, founded in 1683 by Portuguese Jews, the first to migrate to the North American continent. This is the oldest "monument" in New York.

A few blocks away from the cemetery you'll find the **Jewish section** of the Lower East Side. Hester Street is where the market was held at the end of the 19th century. You could buy anything there: religious tracts, kosher meat, jewellery. Go

along the street toward the East River for one block, then take Orchard Street as far as Delancey Street. This will give you a good idea of what Hester Street must have been like. It's one of the most bizarre places in New York. The traders look as though they belong in another world or another century. And there are wonderful bargains to be had. Most of the shops close on Friday afternoons and all day Saturday for the sabbath. Sunday is the day to go, when Greek shish kebab venders and black poker players rub shoulders with crowds of Puerto Ricans and Orthodox Jews in their fur hats and black frock coats.

Despite their poverty, Jewish immigrants managed to found an incredible number of synagogues, several theatres and numerous bookshops and publishing firms here. The area has been on the decline since the 1920s, but most of the synagogues remain. There are plenty of delicatessens and dairy restaurants where you can sample Jewish-style food.

Retrace your steps as far as Hester Street and turn west. Cross the Bowery (see p. 53) to reach **Little Italy,** the third of the so-called ethnic quarters on Lower East Side. But in contrast to the other two, Little

48

Italy is now first and foremost a tourist centre. Most of the houses have been renovated and smart restaurants are gradually taking over from the little *trattorie*, caterers are ousting old grocery stores. In fact it's now a pretty good place in which to eat. Not all the restaurants are excellent, and you'll often see long queues outside the best, but the terraces are very pleasant. There's nothing special to see in Little Italy. Mulberry Street is the main street of the neighbourhood and the most lively. The Feast of San Gennaro takes over here in September (see p. 87).

Greenwich Village and SoHo

It's fashionable to claim that the Village is no longer what it was. But the same could be said of any place in vogue for a while. Though it's overrun by fashion boutiques and candlelit restaurants with chequered table cloths, Greenwich Village remains one of the prettiest parts of New York—as well as the most casual and animated.

Start your tour in **Washington Square** at the end of Fifth Avenue, the heart of the New York University campus. This is the largest private university in the United

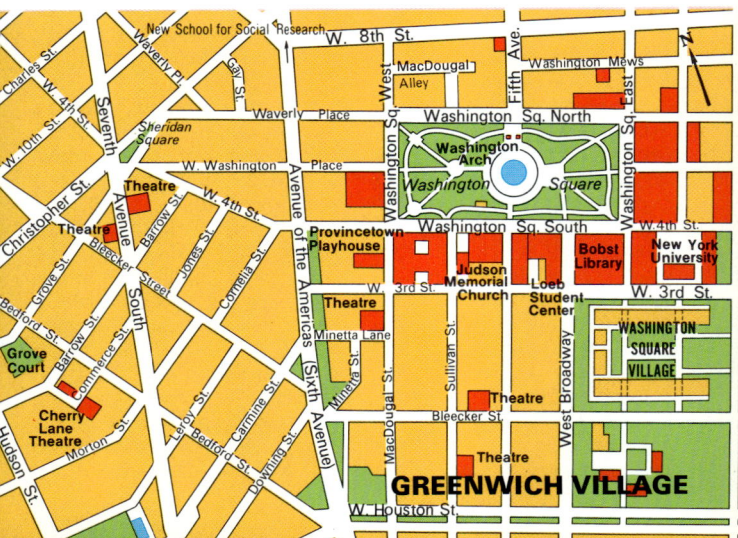

States. By day you can cross the park to admire the view up Fifth Avenue through the famous **Washington Arch** designed by architect Stanford White. It was built in 1889 to commemorate the 100th anniversary of Washington's inauguration as president. The park boasts New York's oldest tree, on oak which for many years served as a gallows. Twenty highwaymen were hanged from it in 1824 in "honour" of Lafayette's visit to New York.

At night it's wiser to keep out of the square, a busy centre for drug trafficking.

Washington Square is surrounded by university buildings—classrooms and student residences. The very attractive houses on the north side are rented to professors. All the narrow streets to the south merit a visit. The most animated are MacDougal and Bleecker, teeming with restaurants, jazz cellars and craft shops.

There are many cafés in this area serving good espresso coffee. Go west along Bleecker Street until you reach Sixth Avenue; follow it to the north, as far as 4th Street, one of the main shopping streets in the Village. A short way along you will come to Sheridan Square,

Originality of shops and costumes brightens the Greenwich Village scene.

where you go left on Christopher Street into a choice residential area. Small tree-lined streets of "brownstones" —similar-looking, four-storey brick or brownish-red sandstone houses, each with a flight of stairs leading up to the door—make up this perfectly charming neighbourhood. You'll find the Village's best antique dealers here and some very good restaurants. The streets around Christopher have almost a country feel to them.

Retrace your steps as far as Sheridan Square and follow Waverly Place back to Washington Square. Then go up MacDougal towards 8th Street. **MacDougal Alley** and, on the other side of Fifth Avenue, **Washington Mews** are two lovely lanes banned to traffic that used to lead to the stables belonging to Washington Square's wealthy inhabitants. Come back to the Avenue of the Americas and walk down Greenwich Avenue, with its hodgepodge of little **51** shops and fine art and poster galleries.

You should really make two trips to the Village: once during the day to see the sights, and a second time at night to get a feel for the atmosphere, have dinner and listen to some jazz or folk music.

SoHo, short for South of Houston, is the area to the south of West Houston Street (generally regarded as the southern limit of the Village). After a long period as an abandoned industrial district, SoHo has become quite chic. Artists who can no longer afford the rents in the Village have resettled here, taking over lofts or warehouse floors. The wealthier ones have installed kitchens and bathrooms and hired the best interior decorators to do their apartments. The homes of the poorest have remained warehouses—with no modern conveniences, but plenty of space and light. No one has curtains, so in the evenings you can look in through the enormous lighted windows and see what the interiors are like. The main street of SoHo, West Broadway, has all the avant-garde galleries. The four best known are located at No. 420, where they show both unknown artists and established stars like Andy Warhol, Robert Rauschenberg and Roy Lichtenstein. New galleries open up almost every day, and if you come on Saturday you'll rub shoulders with New York's intelligentsia. SoHo, which until recently was quite authentic, is now becoming too well known and overrun, just like the Village—which in no way detracts from its charm. But young artists are already thinking of moving out as the rents move up.

The **East Village** is situated east of Washington Square. Purists claim it is the *real* Village, but in fact it is a rundown, somewhat depressing neighbourhood that still has enough interesting sights to merit a brief visit. On Lafayette Street level with Astor Place you can see what remains of a group of marble-pillared Greek Revival houses known as **Colonnade Row.** In the mid-19th century, this was the smartest address in town. The building opposite, which once housed the first public library, is now the headquarters of Joseph Papp's **Public Theater,** a group of avant-garde theatres. The shows presented in the auditoriums here are always of very high quality. Quite often a play will be tried out at the Public Theater before moving on to Broadway.

Astor Place leads onto the **Bowery**, a street laid out by Peter Stuyvesant in the 17th century to his farm (*bouwerij* in Dutch). Last century this was New York's "grand boulevard" lined with dance halls and beer taverns. These days it's mostly given over to sordid hotels and drunks in the last stages of alcoholism. But there are some good rock and jazz spots and theatres have moved in. You needn't be afraid to go there in the evening: the Bowery is much less dangerous than it looks.

Uptown

The Upper West Side is the area of Manhattan west of Central Park. It's a lively mixed-up district, the part of town that can claim most success in racial integration. Here a hodge-podge of intellectuals and artists live side by side with shopkeepers and bus drivers of different ethnic and racial backgrounds. There are old New Yorkers who "wouldn't let wild horses" drag them away from their neighbourhood. And indeed, they'd be quite wrong to move since the West Side, which has seen some bad years, is now getting better day by day.

Lincoln Center

It was construction of the Lincoln Center for the Performing Arts, between 62nd and 66th Streets west of Broadway, that launched the revival of this neighbourhood. In 1955 John D. Rockefeller III put forward the proposal for a great cultural centre to house the Metropolitan Opera, the New York Philharmonic, the New York City Ballet and the Juilliard School of Music. The city bought the land and razed the Puerto Rican ghetto on the site. Financed entirely by private funds, the Center covers an area of some 12 acres. The plaza, an esplanade surrounding a fountain where open-air shows are put on in summer, is the focal point for the three major buildings, each designed by a different architect to blend harmoniously with the others.

To the left of the plaza is the **New York State Theater,** home of the New York City Ballet and the New York City Opera. Designed by Philip Johnson and built in 1964, it has a simple, stately façade, but a lush, red and gold auditorium studded with crystal.

The **Metropolitan Opera House** (the "Met"), designed by Wallace K. Harrison and completed in 1966, can hold 3,800 people. It is the most beautiful building in the complex, with its airy front of glass highlighted by marble pillars, reminiscent of American colonial style. Two Chagall frescoes adorn the central lobby and can be seen from the outside.

Facing the New York State Theater is Avery Fisher Hall, completed in 1962, more commonly known as **Philharmonic Hall.** The auditorium, which seats 2,836, now has excellent acoustics. The New York Philharmonic and distinguished visiting orchestras and soloists play here.

Just behind the hall, level with the Met, you can see the outline of the **Vivian Beaumont Theater,** designed by the great architect Eero Saarinen who died before its completion in 1965. The Beaumont is the new home of the New York Shakespeare Festival. In addition to the delightful circular theatre, there is the second, much smaller Mitzi Newhouse Theater. The building was originally intended to provide a base for a permanent American repertory company, along the lines of the Comédie Française in Paris, but the company never materialized.

Behind the Vivian Beaumont is the **Library and Mu-**

seum of the Performing Arts, a public library housing thousands of records and books about the arts.

Further back, but connected to Lincoln Center by a footbridge over 65th Street, you'll find the **Juilliard School,** one of the world's outstanding conservatories of music. Alice Tully Hall on the ground floor is a concert hall where the best pupils often perform in the free afternoon concerts. It is also the home of the Chamber Music Society.

Guided one-hour tours around Lincoln Center start at the concourse level of the Metropolitan Opera House at frequent intervals (see also p. 120).

Henry Moore sculpture looms over romantic couple at Lincoln Center.

Central Park

A vast green breathing space in the centre of Manhattan (half a mile wide and two and a half miles long), Central Park is sports field, playground and picnic spot for tens of thousands of city-dwellers. In the 1840s, the poet William Cullen Bryant realized that New York needed more parks for its rapidly expanding population. He launched a campaign to persuade the city to buy the land—then wasteland inhabited by squatters—beyond the city limits. Frederic Law Olmsted and Calvert Vaux, landscape gardeners, were called upon to design the park. It took 3,000 workers 20 years to complete it. Conceived

Matched pair of cyclists catch their breath on Central Park lawn.

in the English style, the park doesn't really look man-made. The lake, the "forests", the paths and meadows might have been there since time immemorial. The 75,000 trees, flourishing despite the shortage of soil and the abundance of rocks, are home to countless half-tame squirrels.

By day it's perfectly safe to go walking in the park, at least as far north as 95th Street. But avoid the area in the evenings (unless you're going to the outdoor summer theatre). The **zoo** at the southern end of the park (64th Street and Fifth Avenue) is not always very clean, so on hot days it can be pretty smelly, but the kids love it. Behind the zoo is the **Mall,** a wide tree-lined promenade leading to the **Bethesda Fountain**—on Sundays the scene of an Oriental market. Beyond the fountain is a pretty lake where you can hire rowing boats; nearby are statues of Hans Christian Andersen and Alice in Wonderland. Further north, on a level with the Metropolitan Museum, is **Cleopatra's Needle,** a 3,000-year-old obelisk that was a gift from Egypt in the late 19th century.

The reservoir a little further on has become the rallying spot for New Yorkers who like to play football in the evenings. In fact the park is quite a paradise for active sports lovers (see pp. 88–90). There is something going on every day, but most of all on Sundays in the summer. Miles of bicycle and bridle paths are found in the park, along with tennis courts, an ice-skating rink, a pond for sailing model boats and adventure playgrounds for children.

Free open-air concerts and operas are presented in the **Sheep Meadow** during the summer months.

The **Delacorte Theater,** south of 81st Street on the West Side of the park, is the place to see the excellent "Shakespeare in the Park" festival. Also free, but you must line up ahead of time for tickets.

Columbia University Area

Located on Amsterdam Avenue and 112th Street, **St. John the Divine** is "the world's largest Gothic-style cathedral." Begun in 1892 and almost completed by 1939, much remains to be done if the original plans are respected. Inside this Episcopalian cathedral are some beautiful tapestries, paintings by 16th-century Italian masters and several icons. Immediately behind the cathedral, you come to the campus of **Columbia University.** Founded in 1754 as King's **57**

College, by King George II, Columbia is a member of the Ivy League, that very exclusive club of old American universities which includes Yale, Princeton and Harvard. Dwight D. Eisenhower was its president for a while. The law school, the departments of political science and education and the school of journalism all enjoy excellent reputations. You can wander around the campus quite freely. The Pantheon-like building with the monumental stairway on the north end of the central campus is the Low Memorial Library.

The university is private and therefore fee-paying, but its income from the rent for Rockefeller Center enables it to offer a number of scholarships. The university outgrew its actual campus some time ago and now owns most of the apartment houses in the neighbourhood.

In Riverside Park at 122nd Street stands **Grant's Tomb,** the mausoleum of General Ulysses S. Grant, Commander-in-Chief of the Union Army in the Civil War and United States president from 1869 to 1877. Open Wednesday through Sunday.

Beside the park is **Riverside Drive,** lined with apartment houses that started life in the luxury class, then were out of fashion for a while, but are once again very much in demand. If you want to get a good idea of life in a New York neighbourhood, walk back along Broadway until you're tired, then take the subway to your hotel.

Harlem

"If you haven't seen Harlem, you haven't seen New York," proclaim real lovers of the town. Tourists who want to see the city's underside for themselves should follow certain ground rules: do not go there alone or in too large a group; wear fairly inconspicuous clothing; take as little money as you can get by with, no jewellery, and above all, don't carry a camera; stick to the main shopping streets (especially 125th); take a taxi so you can avoid the sparsely populated, hence more dangerous, streets; and, lastly, don't go there at night.

Probably the best way to visit Harlem is with a guided tour. There are two agencies run by blacks who want to show their community to outsiders, concealing neither the best features nor the worst. You must book with them the previous day: "Penny Sightseeing Company" (tel. 247-2860) and

"Harlem Spirituals, Inc." (tel. 944-9110).

Harlem starts at 110th Street, at the northern end of Central Park, and stretches as far as 162nd Street. Just a few years ago it was the home of a million blacks from the South and the Caribbean islands. Today there are barely half a million. Optimists attribute this exodus to new housing programmes and the improvement in living standards among black people. The pessimists counterclaim that the poor have been forced out of Manhattan by the increasing dilapidation of their ghetto, and have only gone as far as outlying districts such as the South Bronx, which has become a second Harlem. There's some truth in both arguments.

Founded by Dutch settlers, Harlem remained a village for a long time. Not until the end of the 19th century, at the time of the huge wave of immigrants, was it assimilated into the town. Since the newcomers settled on the Lower East Side, middle-class Americans decided to put a gap between themselves and these ill-bred, noisy people. A lot of families built second residences in Harlem, then a purely residential district, and some traces of its former glory can still be seen on the building façades.

Black people started moving in around 1910, the beginning of the Jazz Age, those wild years that came to a peak about 1930. New York was the "Promised Land" for southern blacks, who found untold freedom here. Duke Ellington and Cab Calloway played the Cotton Club and the Apollo, drawing crowds of white people up to Harlem.

It's difficult today to picture what those years must have been like. The Apollo is still there, but it's no more than a shadow of its former self (though plans are afoot to build it up again into a great centre of jazz) and Harlem looks like a bombed-out city. The process of destruction is pitifully simple: tenants get behind on rent payments and on gas and electricity bills. These services are cut off, shortly followed by the water supply. Winter comes, pipes freeze, then burst. Life becomes impossible. But the municipality can only rehouse the homeless. So, inevitably, somebody sets fire to the block: it's the only way of getting into some warm place for the winter. The building stays there, a blackened shell, until it is about to collapse. In the end, it will be torn down leaving behind an ugly gap.

But some nice streets remain, particularly around Edgecombe Avenue, an area peopled by wealthy blacks who could afford to move away but have stayed out of solidarity. That's where you'll find the **Morris-Jumel Mansion** (Edgecombe and W. 160th Street), a stately house set in a garden, one of New York's last reminders of the Georgian architecture of colonial days. Built in 1765 and used during the American Revolution as George Washington's headquarters, it was bought in 1810 by Stephen Jumel, a wine merchant from France. The third vice president, Aaron Burr, married Jumel's widow and lived here for a time.

The interior is now beautifully restored with a lot of period furniture, particularly French, that belonged to the Jumels or is associated with them. For opening times, see p. 120.

Religion has always played an important part in the lives of black Americans. The Black Muslims have flourished in recent years, and there are numerous evangelical Protestant sects, many unknown elsewhere, that have transformed some ancient movie houses into "pop" temples. Try to attend one of these services. Choose one of the churches around Edgecombe Avenue and ask the minister if the congregation would object to your presence. You simply must stay for coffee after the service if you don't want to offend your hosts. And don't forget to put on your Sunday best. White Americans are not always welcome, but Europeans have a better reputation among these blacks and are almost sure to be received kindly.

The east side of Harlem is now largely the domain of Puerto Ricans. It's even known as Spanish Harlem. You can quite safely visit the covered market under the railroad (Park Avenue from 111th to 116th Streets). Everything there—the crowds, the music, the smells—seems to belong more to Mexico or the Caribbean than the United States. You can buy mangoes, papayas, sugar cane, rosaries "blessed by the pope," powders against the evil eye, plants inducing abortion and love potions. The market is open every day but most active on Saturdays. You'll pay less if you can speak a few words of Spanish.

In mild weather local life moves outdoors in crowded Harlem.

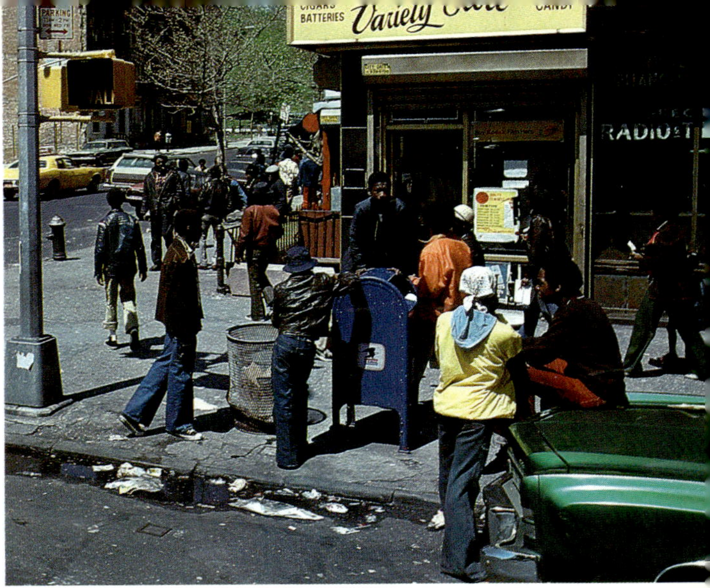
PARKING
BATTERIES
Variety
RADIO

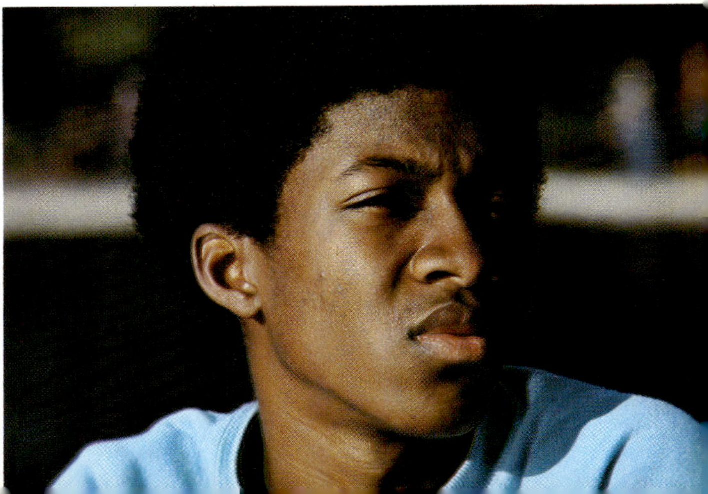

Museums

The museums alone make New York one of the world's great cultural capitals. At last count, there were 120. Visiting just a few of them could easily fill up your entire visit. Here's a brief description of the major ones, in order of importance. For your convenience, museum opening times are grouped under SIGHTSEEING HOURS, pp. 119–121.

Metropolitan Museum of Art. Fifth Avenue at 82nd Street.

A world in itself, the "Met" has nearly 250 rooms, over 4,500 paintings and drawings, one million prints, 4,000 objects from the Middle Ages and so on. You have a simple choice: either you confine your visit to the rooms that particularly interest you—or you stay forever.

In the basement is the Junior Museum, a well-planned introduction to art for children; a shop selling posters of special exhibitions and reproductions; and the Costume Institute, with one of the largest collections in the world. It puts on a special exhibit every year.

As you enter the lobby on the main floor, you will doubtless admire the wonderful arrangements of fresh flowers—the legacy of a rich American who left her money to the museum specifically for this purpose.

On the left are the Greek and Roman rooms, to the right, Egyptian art, featuring a tomb you can walk into. Straight ahead behind the stairway you'll find the marvellous **medieval collection.** Don't miss it if you're there at Christmas time when they set up a gigantic tree decorated with medieval wooden figurines. Along the sides are a Renaissance patio, the decorative arts and European furniture rooms, and the armory. Then at the west end you'll come to a newly built annex which houses the fabulous **Lehman Collection,** displayed in an exact replica of the rooms where the donor had enjoyed these works of art. You will see medieval pieces and magnificent Italian primitives alongside an excellent group of Impressionist paintings.

Thirty-five rooms on the second floor are devoted to **European painting** from the 15th to the 20th centuries. This entire book would not be sufficient to describe all the paintings. The wealth of the collection is simply beyond imagination. Rembrandt, Rubens, Giotto, Veronese, Bosch, Vermeer, El Greco, Velázquez, Corot, Monet, Manet, Cé-

The New York School

Until the late 1930's American art was largely derivative of European work. But in the years preceding the Second World War, some of Europe's most distinguished avant-garde artists—Léger, Mondrian, Hans Hofmann and Max Ernst to name a few—settled in New York. They made an immediate and decisive impact on the cultural environment of the city, fostering the development of America's first truly innovative school of painting, the so-called New York school of abstract expressionists.

JACKSON POLLOCK (1912–56) pioneered the technique of action painting, applying paint directly to the canvas in splashes and dribbles, sometimes without the aid of brushes. As a result, his pictures took on a new and startling immediacy.

FRANZ KLINE (1910–62) was a stellar figure in the abstract expressionist movement, creating works of seminal importance in the 1950's and 60's. He generally kept to a palette of black, white and grey.

WILLEM DE KOONING (born 1904) took up the technique of action painting mid-way in his career. Unlike other members of the New York school, de Kooning's work crosses the boundary between the abstract and realist, e.g. his series of painting entitled *Woman*.

MARK ROTHKO (1903–70) developed a highly original style characterized by the interplay of horizontal bands of colour.

MARK TOBEY (1890–1976) was profoundly marked by his study of Oriental calligraphy, and some of his best-known pictures are referred to as "white writing". Although his approach was much more disciplined than Pollock's, there are many affinities in the work of the two.

zanne, Degas, Van Gogh are just some of the masters represented here.

On the same floor you'll discover a display of musical instruments from all over the world. You can hire a cassette recorder and hear how each instrument sounds. The rest of the floor is taken up by Far Eastern art, a beautiful collection of Islamic art, the American wing—paintings, sculpture and furniture—and rooms for special exhibitions.

And the museum continues to grow: a gallery has been opened for the Temple of Dendur, a gift from Egypt that was brought over and reconstructed stone by stone in the museum's workshops.

Museum of Modern Art. 11 West 53rd Street.

Designed by Philip Goodwin and Edward Durell Stone (the two wings by Philip Johnson), the MOMA, as it's affectionately known, is devoted to "works of art from 1880 to 1950." Though not a museum of avant-garde art, it frequently presents exhibits of contemporary artists. There are over 25,000 works in the museum's vaults, but only a small portion of the collection is on view at any one time and you can see it all easily in one visit.

Go into the garden—in summer it's a cool haven as well as the setting for sculptures by Renoir, Rodin, Maillol, Picasso, Moore and Calder. In the adjoining cafeteria, they serve quite decent sandwiches and snacks.

Temporary exhibitions and recent acquisitions appear on the ground floor. The second floor is devoted to the forerunners of contemporary art. The display may vary, but you will certainly find canvases by Henri Rousseau, by Impressionists and post-Impressionists, by "Nabis" and Fauvists, by Cubists and Expressionists. You will see Monet's lovely *Water Lilies*, works by Italian Futurists and geometric abstracts. The Philip L. Goodwin Gallery contains contemporary furniture and household objects of outstanding design.

The highlight of the third floor is Picasso's ironic and tender *Les Demoiselles d'Avignon*. It's equally famous neighbour, *Guernica*, left the MOMA in September 1981

Whitney Museum concentrates on works by United States' artists.

after over 40 years of safe-keeping at the artist's request. (It is now on view at the Prado, Madrid.)

The work of Dadaists, Surrealists, Abstract Expressionists, some sculptures and a prodigious photography section fill the rest of the third floor.

As you leave the museum, spare a few moments for "Bookstore 2" run by MOMA, two doors to the west; it sells some of the articles on display in the design section, plus posters, books about art and the loveliest greeting cards you've ever seen.

During the summer season, concerts are given in the museum garden.

Other Major Museums

Guggenheim Museum, Fifth Avenue at 89th Street. Free Tuesday evenings after 5.

The first thing to notice about the Guggenheim is the

building. Some call it a giant snail, other pronounce it a masterpiece of New York architecture. Its architect, Frank Lloyd Wright, regarded it as a piece of sculpture. Inside, a wide spiral ramp—the gallery—runs around the wall. The sky-lit core is empty. The incline, the colour of the wall, the lighting have all been carefully selected so that the viewer's eyes do not tire.

The basic collection is that of Solomon R. Guggenheim, who came here from Switzerland and made his fortune in copper. His collection has since been enlarged to include works by Kandinsky, Klee and Chagall, plus thousands of others. The Justin K. Thannhauser collection, housed in an annex, contains paintings by Renoir, Monet, Cézanne, Van Gogh, Gauguin and Degas. The museum holds 8 to 12 different exhibitions each year.

Visitors can eat in the attractive cafeteria (with a covered terrace for summer dining) and the bookshop has a wide choice of posters and books for sale.

Frick Collection, 1 East 70th Street. Children from 10 to 16 with adult only; no children under 10 admitted.

Henry Clay Frick, also of Swiss origin, was a steel magnate who, like other American multi-millionaires of the early 20th century, set aside part of his fortune for acquiring works of art. The museum used to be his home, so you can get some idea of how rich New Yorkers used to live.

There is an 18th-century French boudoir with 8 panels commissioned from François Boucher by Madame de Pompadour; a Fragonard salon containing an assortment of fine pieces; the dining room has portraits by Hogarth, Reynolds and Gainsborough; other treasures include El Greco's *St. Jerome as Cardinal,* Holbein portraits, *Philip of Spain* by Velázquez, *Education of the Virgin* by de La Tour, Dutch landscapes, some striking full-length portraits by James Whistler, and three splendid Rembrandts. The carpets, the furniture and the exhibits are all priceless. You can attend chamber music concerts on Sundays in winter; write in advance for the free tickets. The concerts are held in one of the most charming areas of the museum, the glass-domed, marble-floored courtyard with its pool and fountain.

Whitney Museum of American Art, Madison Avenue at 75th Street. Free admission Tuesday evenings.

The Whitney, entirely devoted to American art, was just an annex of the Museum of Modern Art until 1966. It's worth visiting for Marcel Breuer's building, in the shape of an inverted pyramid, as well as for the collection.

Every two years a special exhibition is held to introduce young American artists. The Whitney's curators have a reputation for being the most dynamic and imaginative in New York. There's also a branch of the Whitney midtown in the Philip Morris building (Park Avenue and 42nd Street), featuring permanent and changing exhibitions.

Cloisters, Fort Tryon Park. (This is a branch of the Metropolitan Museum of Art.)

Once again it is a millionaire, John D. Rockefeller, Jr., whom we have to thank for this museum, a strange concoction of medieval ruins brought from France, Italy and Spain and reassembled as a fortified monastery. Many Europeans are shocked to see "their" cloisters reconstructed on the banks of the Hudson.

There are some lovely things here including the chapel of San Martín de Fuentidueña from Segovia; the Romanesque cloister of St. Michel-de-Cuxa from the Pyrenees; the cathedral treasury; the Unicorn and Burgos tapestries; and the famous Mérode triptych. In the pretty garden, filled with medicinal herbs used in the Middle Ages, concerts are presented during the summer.

American Museum of Natural History, Central Park West at 79th Street.

This is the largest natural history museum in the world, and most of the rooms have remarkable displays. Be sure to see the section on minerals and precious stones, featuring the "Star of India", the largest sapphire ever found, alongside moonstones and other gems.

Dinosaur exhibits fill two of the great halls. There are some marvellous rooms devoted to Africa, but you may be disappointed by the Mexican and Latin American sections, though they do have some superb jewellery. There's something here from every continent, covering the whole of the animal kingdom and many primitive civilizations. The Gardner D. Stout Hall of Asian Peoples, the museum's largest permanent anthropological exhibition, depicts life in Asia from the Peking man to the 19th century.

Next door is the **Hayden Planetarium,** known for its sparkling programmes about **67**

Awesome dinosaur skeletons at Natural History Museum always rouse school-children's curiosity.

the stars and space exploration. The **Laserium** (same building) has sound and light shows featuring the laser beam three or four evenings a week.

Cooper-Hewitt Museum, at Fifth Avenue and 91st Street. Free on Tuesday evenings.

This is the latest of the great New York museums. Located in the sumptuous mansion built for Andrew Carnegie in 1900, it owns the largest collection of decorative art in the U.S. Special exhibitions with unusual themes are held regularly.

Brooklyn Museum, 188 Eastern Parkway, Brooklyn. Free admission.

This museum is outside Manhattan but well worth visiting, for two reasons: first, it's the only one of its kind, and, second, it overlooks Prospect Park where you can spend a very pleasant afternoon if you're tired of the city. You can get there without too much trouble on the IRT No. 2 or 3 express subway from Times Square. The trip to the nearest station (Eastern Parkway) takes about half an hour.

The pre-Columbian art alone is worth the detour.

But the sections devoted to Egyptian, Far Eastern and Persian art are also remarkable. The costume museum is lovely, and the remaining rooms house a permanent exhibition of American furniture from the time of the first settlers to the present day.

What's more, you can purchase craft objects here from around the world at unbeatable prices.

More Museums

International Center of Photography, Fifth Avenue and 94th Street. Library, exhibition galleries and laboratories.

Intrepid Sea-Air-Space Museum, Pier 86, West 46th Street and 12th Avenue. World War II-era aircraft carrier. Extensive exhibits and evocative audio-visual presentations.

Jewish Museum, Fifth Avenue at 92nd Street. Jewish ceremonial objects, archaeological remains from the Holy Land, coins.

Museum of American Folk Art, 49 West 53rd Street. Historical and contemporary folk arts.

Museum of the American Indian, Audubon Terrace, Broadway at 155th Street. The world's largest collection of Indian art and artefacts of **69**

North, Central and South America.

Museum of the City of New York. Fifth Avenue and 104th Street. (See p. 99.)

Museum of Holography, 11 Mercer Street, SoHo. First museum of its kind in the world featuring holograms (pictures developed by laser light creating three-dimensional images).

New-York Historical Society, 170 Central Park West, between 76th and 77th streets. Important museum and research library for American history.

Pierpont Morgan Library, Madison Avenue and 36th Street. Rare books, illuminated manuscripts, Old Master paintings, Florentine sculpture, etc., amassed by the American industrialist J. Pierpont Morgan.

South Street Seaport Museum, East River, at the foot of Fulton Street. Restored seaport area of 19th-century buildings and sailing ships (see pp. 45–46).

And finally, a museum that isn't quite a museum: **The New York Experience,** in the McGraw-Hill Building, Avenue of the Americas and 49th Street. Shows featuring the history of New York on 16 screens, with 45 projectors and quadraphonic sound.

Excursions

The Statue of Liberty* and Ellis Island

For millions of immigrants the Statue of Liberty, or more simply "the Lady," was their first glimpse of America, a symbol of the New World. Americans still value it above all other monuments.

The ferry to the statue on Liberty Island leaves from Battery Park on the southern tip of Manhattan (for times, see p. 120). The crossing takes about 20 minutes. Get there ahead of time if you want a seat on the upper deck.

Make the trip on a good day. The crossing is wonderful and you'll have a magnificent view of Wall Street and downtown Manhattan. Once on the island, go first to the **American Museum of Immigration** inside the base of the statue and avoid the crush at the elevators.

The museum, which was opened in 1972, briefly retraces, through multi-media exhibits, the history of the main national groups responsible for the creation of the United States. It's a sign of the times that emphasis is given to the

---

* Renovations under way due to finish 1986—check before visiting.

contributions of blacks and Indians, the only Americans for whom the statue has no historical signification.

When you've seen enough of the museum, you can choose between climbing the 167 stairs to the top of the pedestal, or paying to ride up in the elevator. If you can face it, there are 12 more stories to climb to the platform inside the Lady's crown, where the **view** is simply fantastic.

The Statue of Liberty, the

Ferryboat passengers admire the most American of monuments, still beckoning from island in harbour.

work of sculptor Frédéric-Auguste Bartholdi, was a gift from France to the United States in recognition of the friendship between the two countries which dates back to the American Revolution.

The project cost $250,000, took 10 years to complete and aroused interest throughout the world. Not a day went by without some curious visitor dropping in to see Bartholdi in his studio. The completed statue which towered above the houses of Paris, had to be taken apart again and shipped over in 214 cases. It was officially unveiled by President Cleveland on October 28, 1886. The 300-foot statue (including the pedestal) attracts millions of visitors each year.

A short way beyond Liberty Island on the ocean side lies **Ellis Island,** which played a rather special role in the history of America. More than half the immigrants who arrived between 1892 and 1924, that is, some 12 million people, went through screening here to be turned back or allowed to enter the New World. Before Americans set up consular missions abroad, there was no preliminary selection, and everyone who took passage did so at his own risk. An official in a bad mood, an overconscientious

doctor, or an eye infection contracted on the voyage might cause the hopeful immigrant to be rejected.

The island is now abandoned, and it's hard to picture the painful scenes that took place in these empty, austere buildings. This "island of tears" has been declared a historical monument and was opened to the public in 1976. A ferry runs from Battery Park, leaving three or four times a day from May to October.

Boat and Helicopter Excursions

Your visit to New York would not be complete without the traditional **boat ride around Manhattan.** There's just one company with regular service, the Circle Line, leaving from Pier 83 on the Hudson River at West 43rd Street (see BOAT EXCURSIONS, p. 106). You may want to combine this outing with a visit to the museum-ship *Intrepid,* docked at Pier 86 (see p. 69).

The boat goes round the island of Manhattan, a 35-mile voyage that takes three hours. It's quite a long trip, but well worth doing. A guide will indicate points of interest. To see Manhattan in a boat in a shorter period of time, take the **ferry to Staten Island** from Battery Park.

Flying over the town in a **helicopter** is an unforgettable

Sailor's view of Brooklyn Bridge.

New York's Best Bridges

Water-laced New York has 65 bridges to hold it together, 14 that connect the isle of Manhattan with the surrounding area.

The 1,595-foot **Brooklyn Bridge** created a sensation when it opened in 1883. But it was plagued by misfortune from the start. Its engineer, John Roebling, died in the early phases of the project as a result of an accident, and his son Washington, who carried on the work, was paralyzed by the bends contracted in the course of the job. And they were not the only casualties. Nonetheless the bridge with its wire webbing is a beautiful success and a favourite subject for photographers and Sunday painters.

The double-decker **George Washington Bridge** spans the Hudson between Manhattan and New Jersey. Designed by O.H. Ammann, its graceful lines show up best at night when the bridge is illuminated.

Newest on the New York horizon is one of the world's longest suspension structures (4,260 feet), the **Verrazano-Narrows Bridge** from Brooklyn to Staten Island, also the work of Ammann. It's named after the Italian who discovered New York Bay in 1524, landing near the bridge's Staten Island base.

Neighbourhood life is preserved in Brooklyn Heights, within sight of Manhattan's skyscraper towers.

experience. There are various tours available, starting off at a very reasonable price. The shortest flight lasts only five minutes and doesn't go beyond the United Nations area. The longest shows you the whole town. It's probably best to choose one in between, on which you can see the World Trade Center, Midtown Manhattan and Central Park.

There are departures throughout the day. You may have to wait a while around midday at peak tourist season. Flights leave either from the East River at 34th Street (Island Helicopter: tel. 683-4575) or from the Seaplane Terminal at the end of East 23rd Street (Pelham Airways: tel. 828-0420).

For a slightly lower bird's-eye view, try the new **aerial tramway** connecting Manhattan and Roosevelt Island. It leaves from 59th Street and First Avenue.

Brooklyn Heights

Why not go beyond Manhattan at least once for a visit to Brooklyn? With its 2½ million inhabitants, it has a greater population than Manhattan

and indeed is the fourth largest urban centre in America. Brooklynites have a strong pride in their accent and their traditions, and they don't cross over to Manhattan unless they really have to.

Brooklyn Heights on the East River is one of the prettiest neighbourhoods. To get there take the subway (IRT No. 2 or 3) as far as the Clark Street Station. You'll come out in the basement of the **St. George Hotel,** for a time one of the grandest in New York. With its ballroom and sea-water pool, it was considered revolutionary in its day. Little now remains of its past glory.

Outside the hotel turn west along Clark Street. After 3 blocks you will come to an esplanade with one of the most impressive **views** in the world: at your feet are ships unloading their cargoes of sugar and coffee; in front of you is Downtown Manhattan with all its bridges; beyond that, the Bay of New York and the Statue of Liberty. In the late afternoon when the sun is setting the sight will take your breath away.

At the end of the esplanade turn left into **Hicks Street,** a shady street in a quarter that has barely changed since 1860. The brownstones, little red-brick houses, have come back

into fashion and prices here are sky-rocketing. When you reach **Atlantic Avenue,** one of the longest streets in Brooklyn, it's like stepping into another world, a world of Arab restaurants and grocers' stores. Here you can eat very good Egyptian and Lebanese food at prices well below those in Manhattan. On Sundays Atlantic Avenue really bustles with Americans of Middle-Eastern descent who come to do their shopping.

Bronx Park

Still other good reasons for venturing beyond the confines of Manhattan are the **Bronx Zoo,** largest in the United States, and above all the sparkling, newly revamped **New York Botanical Garden Conservatory.** Both are located in Bronx Park. The all-glass conservatory, with a 90-foot-high crystal dome, covers almost an acre. Inside, you will find orchids and palm trees, a gurgling waterfall and the lush aroma of citrus trees. Opening hours are listed on p. 120. Take the IND D or CC train to Bedford Park Boulevard-200th Street. For the zoo, get off at East Tremont Avenue-177th Street on the IRT No. 2 or 5 express subway.

What to Do

Shopping

One of the great joys of New York is window shopping. Just stroll down Fifth Avenue from 59th Street, preferably on a sunny day. You can't help being dazzled by the fabulous jewellery displays, the latest shoes from Paris, luxurious leather goods, books of all nations, houses of beauty, exquisite crystal and porcelain, airline and tourist offices catering to your travel itch, discount stores and, of course, clothes, clothes, clothes. If you're hungry, you'll be able to pick up a giant pretzel along the way.

What to Buy

Bargains. There's always some kind of sale going on in New York. The Sunday papers are filled with ads on current ones. If you don't find what you're looking for, check out the specialized discount shops and the bargain departments of the big stores. Dedicated and experienced bargain-hunters can try their luck on Orchard Street (see p. 48), where they can haggle over the prices.

Cameras, calculators, radios etc. Most of them are Japanese but the price tags reflect New York cut-rate practices.

Clothing. The prodigious array of ready-to-wear clothes will impress all but the most hardened shopper. French designers and American couturiers hang side by side in the high-fashion boutiques. And next door you'll find copies produced for less affluent customers. Visitors from abroad appreciate American men's shirts—well made, low-priced and sized according to neck and sleeve length. They find suits and accessories attractive buys too.

Cosmetics. Shop around the department stores for special bonus offers on your favourite beauty products. Promotion campaigns by the leading firms, featuring free products, make the tour of the town.

Gadgets. In this paradise for gadget-lovers, you can certainly find an original gift to bring home. The best selection appears just before Christmas in speciality shops and the household departments of big stores. Hammacher Schlemmer takes the prize in this category.

Jewellery. Ranging from mass-produced costume jewellery in the very latest styles to the most incredibly elaborate, expensive and original cre- **77**

ations, not forgetting the budget-wise diamond centre on West 47th Street (better if you have an introduction) and hand-made items mostly in silver and copper in Greenwich Village boutiques.

Records and books. Choose from a vast selection of the latest releases in classical, rock, folk, jazz and pop music at discount prices (Discomat, Alexander's and Sam Goody's). You may not listen to the record but are allowed to return it if there is a defect. Best-selling books can be found at somewhat reduced prices, but the real bargains are in items that have been on the shelves for a few years—art books and publications on specialized or off-beat subjects. If you're interested in old or rare books, concentrate on the shops on Fourth Avenue south of 14th Street. Barnes and Noble (Fifth Avenue and 18th Street), one of the world's largest bookshops,

Eye-catching window display fails to distract reflected crowd from fascination of Fifth Avenue parade.

Gallery Promenade

Whether you're in the market for a Miró, a lithograph by a young unknown or simply want to look at pictures, New York's almost 500 galleries await you. Most can be found around Madison Avenue above 60th Street, along 57th Street, in Greenwich Village and in SoHo.

Though the uptown galleries may look very exclusive, they're really open to the public and welcome visitors. Watch for any retrospective or one man shows. SoHo and Village galleries tend to be more down to earth, as are their prices. Some galleries specialize in posters and inexpensive graphics.

now has an uptown store (48th and Fifth Avenue). Customers walk around there with supermarket carts. Other fine bookstores include Doubleday's (largest branch at Fifth Avenue and 56th Street) and Rizzoli International Bookstore (Fifth Avenue and 55th Street).

Sports equipment. Again, a wide choice, expert counsel and discount possibilities in tennis rackets, golf clubs and skis.

Toys. Some brands have a justly deserved reputation for durability. Educational toys abound but you can still find things that are just plain fun. The ultimate toystore is F.A.O. Schwarz (Fifth Avenue and 58th Street), where you can buy a doll's house for $10,000.

Better Avoided

Antiques, whether fake or imported, are exorbitantly priced! Small shops with "Going out of Business" signs in the window that sell cameras, Irish linen, electronic watches and radios;

goods tend to be unreliable and over-priced. Anyone who tries to sell you anything on the street.

Where and When to Shop

As a general rule, stores are open from 10 a.m. to 6 p.m., Mondays to Saturdays. Many shops and department stores open at least one night a week, usually Thursdays. All the large department stores are open Sunday afternoons; boutiques and shops in Greenwich Village open late Saturday night and all day Sunday.

Department stores exist in many shapes and sizes. Starting off with the most interesting: Bloomingdale's (Lexington and 59th Street) is almost a city in itself. A store you absolutely must visit for the most up-to-the-minute clothing, furniture (see their model rooms), accessories, housewares and fine gourmet shop. In fact, just about everything. Macy's (34th Street between Sixth and Seventh avenues), known as the world's largest, does sell everything! Most recent addition, the bright and cheery

In melting-pot area of Lower East Side, advertising techniques of Madison Ave. seem a world away.

Cellar department filled with marvellous food and houseware boutiques.

For fine fashions (especially women's), saunter down Fifth Avenue between 58th and 49th streets stopping at Bergdorf Goodman, Henri Bendel (on 57th Street), Gucci's and Saks Fifth Avenue. Lower down, there's Lord and Taylor's and Altman's, and on 34th Street, Ohrbach's, whose speciality is line-by-line copies of couturier designs. Gimbels, Macy's perennial rival, has two Manhattan branches: one on Sixth Avenue and 33rd Street, the other uptown on East 86th Street.

Men's clothing: most of the above stores have excellent men's shops. But for the world's largest men's clothing store, go to Barney's (Seventh Avenue and 17th Street). Special departments cater to short, tall and rotund customers.

In the discount world, Alexander's (Lexington and 58th Street and Klein's (14th Street at Union Square) offer low-priced clothes and cut-rate prices on appliances and records.

Arcades. Some of New York's most prestigious shops occupy premises in Trump Tower (Fifth Avenue between 56th and 57th streets), next

door to Tiffany's. The building is linked to Bonwit Teller, an elegant department store, and IBM headquarters via a spacious passageway complete with interior waterfall. Citicorp Market (Lexington and 54th Street), features three floors of bright and varied shops.

Nightlife

When the sun goes down and the theatre marquees light up, New York starts moving to another rhythm. A flash tour of the city's nightlife might include some of the following: a brash, exuberant Broadway musical, a dim, smoke-filled room throbbing to a saxophone's wail, block-long queues waiting patiently to see a recent film, elegant champagne-sipping first-nighters at the Met, a tinkling piano playing Gershwin at a forties-style bar, a free concert under the stars on a sweltering July night, and, inevitably, the cool frenzy of the disco dancers. And you haven't even begun to cover the scene. To find out what's on, consult the Friday newspapers or the weekly publications *New York* and *The Village Voice*.

Theatre*

One of the main reasons for visiting New York is to take in a few shows. Broadway means musicals, comedies, conventional drama. But most of the theatres are, physically, off-Broadway, clustered around the sidestreets from West 44th to 50th streets. Broadway has the big stars and the elaborate productions. Tickets for hit shows can be very difficult to obtain at short notice, so it's best to write ahead if you have your heart set on a particular one. Curtain time is usually at 8 p.m., with matinées on Wednesdays, Saturdays and sometimes Sundays. Programmes are free.

Off-Broadway and Off-Off Broadway theatres are scattered all over town. Generally smaller, they can be top-flight or strictly amateur affairs. But the tickets are invariably cheaper. The plays range from revivals of the classics to the most avant-garde theatrical experiments. The Public Theater (425 Lafayette Street), which may have as many as five different productions going at once, can usually be counted on for an interesting evening.

Dance*

When it comes to dance, New York fairly bubbles over with activity. This is headquarters for modern dance, and classical ballet makes a creditable showing too. Between the resident companies—Balanchine's New York City Ballet, Robert Joffrey, Merce Cunningham, Alvin Ailey, The Dance Theater of Harlem, Alwin Nikolaïs and the American Ballet Theatre— and the fine visiting groups which perform here regularly, dance fans are really spoiled.

Opera and Concert*

The city's two major opera companies occupy adjoining buildings in Lincoln Center.

---

* See THEATRE AND CONCERT TICKETS, page 121.

The Met may have the glamour and the Italian tenors but City Opera can lay claim to a more modern and adventurous repertory. Both are superb. As for concerts of classical music, you're likely to find 30 or so scheduled for a single evening—with the New York Philharmonic (also at Lincoln Center) heading the bill. Carnegie Hall, known for its excellent acoustics, plays host to outstanding visiting artists. Free concerts are held frequently at Lincoln Center's Library of the Performing Arts and at the Juilliard School of Music. Summers, the Met and the Philharmonic give free performances in the city's parks.

Cinemas

Every New York neighbourhood has its movie theatres, but the two largest concentrations are in the Times Square area and along Third Avenue above 57th Street. These feature the newest films and the highest prices. Certain cinemas specialize in re-runs of old favourites—like Bogart and W.C. Fields—or in foreign classics. Queuing up outside the theatre can be amusing too—unless of course the weather's miserable. It's a marvellous opportunity to watch the unending, ever-changing parade of people, which is, after all, one of the liveliest aspects of New York nightlife.

The Later Night Scene

The good news is that jazz is coming back. Jazz clubs featuring the old stand-bys as well as newcomers can be found in the Village and SoHo, the West 50s and even the Upper East Side. A special number, Jazzline 463-0200, gives details about who's playing where.

The disco scene is in constant mutation. Yesterday's hottest spot may no longer exist. Just follow the beautiful people dressed in black leather, blue jeans or sequins. Everything goes in clothes, but the more outrageous the better! And don't be surprised at some of the dancing partners. This night scene doesn't really get underway until after midnight.

Yes, you can still find old-fashioned nightclubs and supperclubs in New York. You can dance to sweet music and be entertained in a brassy or silky style. Be prepared to spend. Ethnic nightclubs—Spanish, Israeli, Italian, Greek—vary the scene.

City lights and bustle continue until the wee hours of the morning.

Parades and Festivals

If you don't see a parade during your visit, you'll miss one of New York's most colourful attractions. Every nationality has its own day and scarcely a Sunday goes by (or so it seems) without marching bands and baton twirlers stepping along

Fifth Avenue or some other.

St. Patrick's Day (patron saint of Ireland) on March 17. Fifth Avenue has its centre stripe painted green and the procession lasts all afternoon. Everybody wears some green in honour of Ireland. You'll see more nuns here than in Italy, as well as green-clad majorettes, blue with the cold. Under the benevolent eye of the mounted police (almost all Irish), plenty of alcohol is downed (to ward off the cold, of course).

The **Easter Parade** meanders up Fifth Avenue from St. Patrick's Cathedral. More a promenade than a parade, it's just a lot of people decked out in their spring finery. A good chance to see the best and worst in American fashion.

The **Puerto Rican Day** parade takes place in June. All the island's dignitaries fly into "Nueva York" to participate. Hardly the most orderly procession; in fact it's often quite wild.

The **Columbus Day** parade, on the second Monday in October, is primarily an Italian affair, but the rest of New York turns out to watch.

Fresh-faced girls with pompons go through their earnest paces in patriotic Fifth Avenue parade.

The **Veterans'** parade in November honours those who served in the armed forces.

The **Thanksgiving** parade, on the fourth Thursday of November, marches up Broadway. The big stars are huge, inflated balloons of favourite cartoon characters. This is *the* parade for kids.

Festivals

The **Chinese New Year** is a movable feast occurring in January or February. Go to Chinatown if you're not frightened by the racket—the sidewalks are veritable minefields of firecrackers. They're noisy but harmless.

The **Feast of St. Anthony of Padua** in early June (on Sullivan Street between Houston and Spring streets) and the **Feast of San Gennaro** in September (on Mulberry and Grand streets in Little Italy) both feature fun, games and Italian street food.

The **Newport Jazz Festival** now moves to New York the last week of June. Musicians hold forth in concert halls, in circulating "jazzmobiles" and on the streets. In summer, other open-air festivals take place in Central Park and at Lincoln Center. You can get information on current activities by calling 755-4100.

Sports

Believe it or not, New Yorkers are active sportsmen, and they have more athletic facilities at their disposal than most other city dwellers.

In Central Park you can rent and ride (no cars allowed on weekends) bicycles, hire a boat or even a horse. To play tennis on the city courts you need to buy a season permit, but there are also private indoor and outdoor courts (see the Yellow Pages of the telephone directory) for rent by the hour. Otherwise, you can just follow the example of the thousands of New Yorkers who jog

around the reservoir and along the city sidewalks. In winter there is skating in Central Park (at the Wollman Memorial Rink) and at Rockefeller Center.

New York boasts 18 miles of public beaches with mostly clean if sometimes chilly water. The best, Jones Beach just beyond the city limits on Long Island, is a good 6 miles long. You can always walk away from the crowds who tend to

Despite their sedentary reputation, New Yorkers enjoy cycling, baseball.

settle near the parking areas. To get there, take the Long Island Railroad from Penn Station to Freeport, and then a bus (frequent service in summer) from the station to the beach.

Only a subway (B, QB) ride away is Coney Island in Brooklyn, the birth-place of the hot dog. If you find the beach too crowded or noisy or dirty, wander over to the amusement park.

Armchair sportsmen will find ample fare on television. The major American networks provide excellent coverage of sports events.

The baseball season runs from April to October; football (American style) from September to December. If you want to attend a game, buy your tickets in advance. Ask at the hotel desk or go to a Ticketron (977-9020) outlet. For less important games, you can probably get tickets at the gate. Consult the Friday newspapers for a rundown on the weekend sports activities.

The Mets baseball team and the Jets (football) play in Shea Stadium in Queens, not far from La Guardia Airport. The No. 7 (Flushing IRT) subway, from Grand Central, stops right at the stadium.

The Yankees (baseball) can be seen at Yankee Stadium in the Bronx (161st Street and River Avenue), reached on the No. 4, CC or D subway. The Giants (football team) have moved to the Meadowlands in New Jersey, where soccer is also played.

The important basketball (New York Knicks) and ice hockey (New York Rangers) teams play at Madison Square Garden. The Garden is also the place to see World Championship boxing, horse shows and other assorted sporting events. You may be able to get tickets for individual matches at the Garden's box office.

New Yorkers love to bet on horses. The two big race tracks are Aqueduct and Belmont, both in Queens. The trotters go through their paces at Roosevelt Raceway on Long Island, the Meadowlands and at Yonkers Raceway. Also on Long Island is the Nassau Coliseum, home to the Islanders, New York's ice hockey champions.

The prestigious U.S. Open Tennis Championships, in September, has moved from Forest Hills to Flushing Meadows in Queens.

In a canyon among Radio City's skyscrapers, ice-skaters work out before appreciative passers-by.

Wining and Dining

A stay in New York can be a gastronomic delight. You have your pick of cooking from every corner of the globe—to say nothing of all-American steaks and hamburgers and first-class seafood.

Eating Habits

New Yorkers—resident and transient—seem to operate on staggered schedules. The late riser may see the early lunchers arrive while he's finishing breakfast. You'll find people eating in restaurants almost any time of day.

Breakfast, served between 7 and 11, can consist of juice, toast or Danish pastry (sweet roll) with coffee or tea (Continental breakfast) or the whole works: eggs (served with buttered toast and jam), sausages, pancakes (thick ones coated with maple syrup) or waffles in assorted flavours. English visitors may find American coffee a bit weak and may also be surprised to receive a second cup without asking.

Lunch, from 11.00 to 2.30, usually a hamburger or sandwich washed down with a Coke, iced tea in summer, a glass of iced water or coffee.

Dinner, from 5.30 to 10.30, and often preceded and accompanied by cocktails.

Brunch is a hybrid of breakfast and lunch, traditionally eaten on Sundays. Served any time from 11 to 3, brunch consists of eggs and toast, or whatever else you might fancy. With it you could drink a Bloody Mary (tomato juice and vodka) or some American champagne.

Where to Eat

The main problem is deciding what you want to eat: *linguine* with clam sauce, stuffed cabbage, *canard à l'orange, sauerbraten* with potato pancakes, *moo sho pork, paella, tempura, tacos,* or just "two eggs over easy". You can find it all in New York.

For lunch, no matter where you go it will be crowded. In the evening, avoid the areas around Fifth Avenue and Wall Street—unless you like dining in solitude. It's best to head for the theatre district, Greenwich Village or one of the residential areas (East Side or Upper West Side).

Delicatessens (deli), a cross between grocery stores and restaurants, are known for their gargantuan sandwiches on all kinds of bread, garnished with

They sell no alcoholic drinks and are found all over town.

Take-outs are small shops where you can order an American, Greek, Italian (known as a hero) sandwich, salads, assorted groceries and drinks to take out and eat elsewhere.

Fast food chains. You'll see plenty of reminders that you're in the homeland of McDonald's and Kentucky Fried Chicken. They're very cheap, but you usually eat standing up, or take the food with you.

Pizzerias serve a great variety of enormous Neapolitan-style pizzas, usually big enough for three people. But you can also buy it by the slice.

French restaurants. Approach these with caution, for there are no more than a dozen excellent ones, and another hundred that are mediocre and far too expensive for what they offer.

"Ethnic" restaurants, a term covering all foreign restaurants—Greek, Italian, Japanese, Chinese (and remember that each province has its own style of cooking), Spanish, Mexican, Indian, Middle Eastern, German, Russian, Scandinavian, and so on. There's something for every taste.

huge half-sour (cucumber) or dill pickles; other specialities include salads and hearty soups like mushroom-barley or refreshing cold borscht. Some delicatessens are kosher.

Coffee shops and self-service cafeterias offer hamburgers, French fried potatoes (chips), simple dishes and pastries.

Some of the best Chinese and Italian restaurants are **93**

located in Chinatown and Little Italy. If German or Hungarian food strikes your fancy, head up to Yorkville in the East 80s between Lexington and First avenues. Middle Eastern restaurants can be found on Atlantic Avenue in Brooklyn or—along with Greek, French, Spanish and Filipino cuisine––on Eighth Avenue between 37th and 53rd streets.

Sidewalk cafés have become very popular in recent years. They serve hamburgers, *quiches*, *crêpes* and sandwiches, and will usually let you linger over your coffee.

What to Eat

Sandwiches. Served on white, rye, pumpernickel or wholewheat bread, a roll or a bagel (doughnut-shaped rolls) or the new favourite, *pita*, Arab flat bread. Classic fillings include chicken, tuna and egg salads; lox (smoked salmon) and cream cheese, a delicious Jewish speciality served on a bagel; chopped liver or pastrami (a kind of cured beef), also Jewish specialities; club sandwiches–– three slices of toast filled with lettuce, tomato, bacon and

Picknickers enjoy Central Park's green escape from city's uproar.

sometimes cheese, very high and very hard to get into your mouth; the hot dog, usually served with sauerkraut or fried onions and mustard, was invented in New York; hamburgers, the "national dish", generally much bigger and better than their British equivalents; and grilled cheese, plain or with bacon or tomato.

Soups. These days many Americans will lunch on soup rather than a hamburger, and more and more small restaurants include soups on the menu. Vichyssoise (don't let the name mislead you, it's an American dish) is a chilled concoction of leeks and potatoes and onions; chili con carne, often served as a soup, is in fact a substantial and spicy stew of kidney beans, ground beef, onions and tomatoes.

Salads. Most consist of lettuce, carrots, tomato and cucumber, always chilled. You will be offered a choice of dressings: French, Thousand Islands (mayonnaise, ketchup, hard-boiled egg), Russian (mayonnaise and chili sauce), Italian (oil, vinegar, garlic and herbs) or Roquefort. You can always ask for plain oil and vinegar.

The "chef's salad", which may include ham, cheese and chicken, is a meal in itself; raw **95** spinach salad with mushrooms ranks as a great American original; Caesar salad has romaine lettuce and a raw egg in the dressing; cole slaw (cabbage salad) often appears with sandwiches; Waldorf salad is composed of apples, walnuts and mayonnaise. You'll also find a wide variety of vegetable and fruit salads—often with cottage cheese—specially conceived for weight watchers.

Meat. Beef takes first place. It comes in enormous portions and is almost invariably tender. In steakhouses, you often pay a

flat rate for a steak, a baked potato with sour cream or French fries (chips), a self-service salad bar, and in some cases as much wine, beer or *sangría* as you can drink. Order your steak rare (underdone), medium or well done.

"Spare ribs" are pork ribs, marinated in a spicy sauce, baked or broiled and eaten with your fingers. Ham steak with a slice of pineapple is a speciality from the South. Long Island ducklings are famous for their flavour. Last but not least, stuffed turkey, the holiday favourite, appears on menus year round.

Fish and seafood. It's too often forgotten that New York is an ocean port abounding with fresh seafood. If you like shellfish, then make the most of your stay here. The Long Island Blue Point oysters, subject to strict inspection, are a real delicacy. Oysters and clams on the half-shell come with chili and horseradish sauce and small crackers (biscuits). "Oysters Rockefeller", covered with spinach, sprinkled with breadcrumbs and then browned under a grill are an unexpected but successful combination.

For a change from the perennial shrimp (prawn) cocktail, try soft shell crabs (in spring or summer). You can eat almost

---

Gastronomical Gazetteer

A steak may be a steak any way you slice it, but visitors to the city are sometimes confused by the local terminology.

The tender New York cut, also called shell or strip steak, comes (appropriately) from the tenderloin. London broil did not cross the Atlantic with the pilgrims: it's a native American piece of flank or round cut against the grain. As for Swiss steak, no yodelling please. It's not even steak but braised beef with onion and tomato sauce. When you order minute steak, consult your watch not your ruler. And finally, don't expect anything chummy from club steaks: they come from the rib not select institutions.

every morsel of those crabs caught after they've cast their shells.

Scallops, lobster and Nova Scotia salmon are special treats and much cheaper than their European counterparts.

Fish is good too, usually broiled or deep-fried in batter. Some superstition prompts Americans to chop off the head and tail!

Vegetables. Americans eat lots of salads. If green beans or peas decorate your plate, they're likely to be frozen. In summer, corn on the cob is excellent.

Cheese. Only French restaurants offer a cheese board.

Elsewhere, if you insist, you will be given a slice of "Swiss" or "Dutch" cheese. Vermont cheddar is worth trying for its robust flavour. A recent upsurge in the popularity of cheese has led to great advances in the manufacture of French-style cheeses, particularly those with herbs and garlic.

Desserts. Ice cream comes in a wonderful variety of flavours. Pastries and pies are not always as good, though there are exceptions, including cheesecake and apple pie, topped with a scoop of ice cream (à la mode) or whipped cream, and pumpkin pie, traditionally eaten on Thanksgiving Day. Rice pudding and jello are coffee-shop staples.

In most restaurants you can ask for fresh fruit or fruit salad, which is sometimes offered as a first course.

Drinks. You'll be given a glass of iced water at the start of your meal if you ask for one. Iced tea frequently appears in the warmer months.

Soft drinks are very popular. Cola drinks still lead the market. You can usually get one that is artificially sweetened.

Beer, served ice cold, is comparable to British lager. You can also find pale or brown ale and many foreign beers, either imported or manufactured under licence.

New York State has some decent wines; those from California are even better, especially the white ones. You can order domestic wine by the bottle or, in many places, in carafes as the "house wine". French and Italian wines, at quite reasonable prices, also appear on menus.

Since Americans discovered wine, hard liquor has gone somewhat out of fashion. But not the cocktail hour! Dry martinis (gin and a few drops of dry vermouth) are very potent. Bourbon, mellow whiskey distilled in Kentucky, is made of corn, malt and rye; drink it straight, on the rocks or with soda. Many bars have a late-afternoon "happy hour" when they'll give you two drinks for the price of one or serve free snacks.

Prices

Most restaurants charge more for dinner than for lunch. You can order just a salad if you want, but sometimes there is a minimum charge. Ask about the "special" dish of the day. In simple places, you often pay the cashier on your way out, after leaving the tip on the table. See also TIPPING and Planning Your Budget section.

For Children

Small fry can scamper around in **Central Park's** well-equipped adventure playgrounds, designed to stimulate the imagination. In the southeast corner of the park, visit the Zoo and the Children's Zoo.

Most children absolutely adore the **American Museum of Natural History** (see p. 67) with its skeletons of dinosaurs and stuffed animals displayed in their natural habitats. **Hayden Planetarium** next door puts on a super star show for older (over eight) kids.

The **Museum of the City of New York** (see p. 69) has some wonderful old toys and a special "Touch Everything" section in the New Amsterdam exhibit. During the winter months, there are puppet shows on Saturdays.

The **Metropolitan Museum of Art**'s Junior Museum offers an excellent introduction to the history and enjoyment of art. Visitors are encouraged to push buttons, listen to recordings and look at slides.

Last in this list is the **Museum of the American Indian** (see p. 69), a slightly dusty treasure house of "genuine" possessions of Sitting Bull and other Western heroes.

A trip to New York for any youngster would be incomplete without a visit to the city's most famous toy emporium, **F.A.O. Schwarz** (see p. 79). And of course, many tourist attractions—like boat trips (see p. 73), skyscraper peaks and the South Street Seaport—appeal to all age groups.

Outside of Manhattan there's the mammoth **Bronx Zoo** (see p. 76) and **Coney Island** amusement park in Brooklyn, not recommended for the faint-hearted. A Coney Island excursion could also include the New York **Aquarium** (Surf Avenue and West 8th Street) which features whales, dolphins and a shocking electric eel.

Consult the *New York Times* or *New York* magazine for a detailed listing of special events, theatre and films for children. And if you're going to be in town in the spring, you simply can't miss the "Greatest Show on Earth", Ringling Bros., Barnum & Bailey circus.

How to Get There

From the United States and Canada

BY AIR: There is daily service between New York City and at least one city in every state of the union as well as from Toronto and Montreal. Major U.S. cities are linked with New York by hourly non-stop flights during the day. Fares change constantly, so it would be wise to consult an airline or travel agency for the latest information about discounts and special deals.

BY BUS: The major metropolitan centres in North America have regular bus connections with New York City. The only requirement is that the destination be reached within 60 days after the ticket is purchased. You save approximately 10 per cent on round-trip tickets. Both Greyhound and Trailways offer flat-rate rover passes for specified periods of unlimited travel.

You can also take a scheduled escorted tour to New York City from the South or Midwest. Daily stops allow for sightseeing and meals. Transportation, hotel rooms, baggage handling, sightseeing and admission charges are usually included in the price.

BY RAIL: Amtrak trains, with dining car service and slumber-coach, roomette or bedroom accommodation link New York City with the West Coast.

Amtrak features the U.S.A. Rail Pass for unlimited travel at a flat rate for given periods of time. They also offer package tours to New York which include travel and hotel accommodation.

The Montrealer runs from Montreal to New York, with excellent connections from other parts of Canada.

From the United Kingdom and Eire

BY AIR: Because of the complexity and variability of the many new fares, you need the advice of an informed travel agent well before your holiday. Apart from the standard first-class and economy fares, main types of fares available are:

Super APEX: book 21 days prior to departure for stays of 7 days to 6 months; no stopovers.

Special Economy: book any time; offers plenty of flexibility.

Standby: bookable only on the day of travel, minimum 2 hours prior to departure.

From Australia and New Zealand

From Australia: There's twice-weekly air service from Sydney to New York via Los Angeles. Package deals, excursion fares and APEX fares are available.

From New Zealand: Scheduled flights leave daily for New York from Auckland via Los Angeles. Excursion fares allow intermediate stops. EPIC fares do not permit stopovers.

Baggage allowances and insurance. Travellers to the United States may check in up to two suitcases of unlimited weight, but neither of them may measure more than 62 inches (158 cm.) by 80 inches (203 cm.). It is advisable to insure all luggage for the duration of your trip. Any travel agent can make the necessary arrangements.

When to Go

Between October and March the days are usually clear. In summer you should expect periods of heat and humidity alleviated in part by air-conditioning in shops, hotels and restaurants. Autumn is best for visiting New York, but crisp winter days are not always uncomfortable if you have a heavy coat and boots.

Average monthly day-time temperatures:

	J	F	M	A	M	J	J	A	S	O	N	D
°F	39	41	48	57	70	77	82	81	75	64	53	43
°C	4	5	9	14	21	25	28	27	24	18	12	6

Planning Your Budget

To give you an idea of what to expect, here's a list of average prices in U.S. dollars. They can only be approximate, however, as inflation creeps relentlessly up.

Airport transfer. Taxi from JFK to Manhattan about $25, from La-Guardia $15. Bus from JFK to East Side Terminal or Grand Central Terminal $6, from LaGuardia $4.50. JFK Express $5.

Baby-sitters. $5.50 per hour for one child plus transport.

Bicycles. $3.50 and up per hour, $15 and up for full day.

Buses. 75¢ a trip, including transfer on certain lines (but you must ask for it when you pay). Exact change or a token is required.

Car rental. It's impossible to give a range of average rental charges as prices vary enormously, depending on the season and the firm. Car rental agencies, both international and local, compete furiously for customers, and it's only sensible to shop around and compare offers. The cheaper weekly rates advertised by many companies apply only when a car is reserved a week in advance.

Cigarettes (packet of 20). $1.05 and up.

Entertainment. Cinema $4–$6. Theatre $20–$45 on Broadway, $12–$20 Off-Broadway. Ballet/dance $8–$40. Nightclub $30. Jazz club $15–$20.

Guided tours. $14–$22 bus tour by day. $22–$38 New York by night. Boat trip around Manhattan (Circle Line) $9.50, children $4.50. Walking tours (Central Park, Greenwich Village, SoHo) $1–$6.

Hairdressers. *Man's* haircut $10–$25. *Woman's* haircut $15–$30, shampoo and set $10–$20, shampoo and blow-dry $10–$30, hair colour $15–$50.

Hotels (double room per night). Budget category $45–$65, moderate $70–$90, luxury $125–$275.

Meals and drinks. Breakfast $3–$7, lunch in snack bar $5, in restaurant $10–$15, dinner $15–$35, carafe of wine $6–$7, glass of beer $1.50–$2.50, whiskey $3.50–$5, soft drink 75¢, American coffee $1, espresso $1.50–$3.

Subway. Token 75¢.

Taxis. $1 for first ⅑ mile, 10¢ for each additional ⅑ mile (50¢ surcharge nights and weekends in owner-operated cabs).

Youth hostels (YMCA, per night). Double room with bath $38, single room without bath $20.

BLUEPRINT for a Perfect Trip

An A-Z Summary of Practical Information and Facts

Contents

A star (*) following an entry indicates that relevant prices are to be found on p. 102.

Certain items of information in this section may already be familiar to U.S. residents, but have been included to be of help to visitors from overseas.

A **ACCOMMODATION*.** The New York Convention & Visitors Bureau (see TOURIST INFORMATION OFFICES) can give you an up-to-date list of hotels. You should book a room in advance if possible; the city can be very crowded during convention and holiday periods. Have your reservation confirmed before leaving for New York and bring it along with you. Although prices in New York hotels are not subject to control, they are comparable within similar categories of establishment. Rates are posted in each room, but do not include a tax of 8%. A daily occupancy tax is also added to the bill. Almost all rooms have air-conditioning and television. Unless you are on a pre-paid tour, no meals will be included in the price of the room. At many hotels children can sleep in their parents' room at no extra charge.

A few hotels, like the Martha Washington Hotel, are open only to women. Hotels that cater essentially to businessmen often offer special weekend rates.

Youth hostels. There are no youth hostels as such in New York City, but there are a number of residences run by the YMCA (Young Men's Christian Association) and the YWCA (Young Women's Christian Association), commonly known as Y's. There is no age limit, nor do you have to belong to any special organization to stay in the Y's. But it's better to reserve a room by writing the Resident Director. Two of the best Y's, open to both men and women, are:

Vanderbilt YMCA, 224 East 47th Street, New York, NY 10017 (tel. 755-2410)

Sloane House YMCA, 356 West 34th Street, New York, NY 10001 (tel. 760-5850)

The International Student Hospice at

154 East 33rd Street, New York, NY 10016 (tel. 228-7470)

offers lodging to male students at low rates. A valid student identity card must be shown.

Metropolitan New York Council, American Youth Hostels, Inc.:

132 Spring Street, New York, NY 10012 (tel. 431-7100)

AIRPORTS*. New York is served by three airports—Kennedy, La-Guardia and Newark. Almost all international flights land at Kenne-dy (JFK) airport, where traffic can be very heavy during peak flying times. You may have to circle above New York for a short time before landing. There are a number of terminal buildings, each with its own customs service.

Arriving from abroad, you must first present your passport, the customs declaration form and your landing card to an immigration official. He will attach a temporary residence visa to your passport which must be given back when you leave the country. After you've collected your luggage from the conveyors, you take it through the red or green customs channel, depending on whether you have anything to declare.

Ground transport. Express buses run frequently, about every 20 to 30 minutes, from JFK to the Grand Central Terminal and the East Side Airlines Terminal. From there, you can take a taxi or walk to a city bus stop to get to your destination. If you arrive after dark or have a lot of luggage, take a taxi.

Several companies offer an extremely convenient mini-bus service between the airports and Manhattan hotels. Ring for a ride on the free telephones in the arrivals area; a driver will come around to pick you up within a few minutes. Prices are reasonable and very competitive, so it's worth checking with several firms to get the cheapest fare.

The JFK Express ("Train to the Plane") is a combination of bus and special subway train that stops at eight stations in Manhattan and downtown Brooklyn. The trip takes about one hour, with departure every 20 minutes.

If you prefer to go by taxi, use only the yellow medallioned ones that are licensed by the New York City Taxi Commission.

Regular helicopter service (New York Helicopter) links the airports to each other and to the city heliport on East River (34th Street). Certain airlines offer helicopter service to the 60th and 34th Street heliports; check with your carrier for details.

Departing visitors should arrive at the terminal in good time; during rush hour, it may take more than an hour to reach Kennedy airport. If you go by bus, tell the driver which airline you're flying so he can let you off at the right terminal.

Duty-free shops offer a wide range of articles. Your purchase will be delivered directly to the departure gate where you'll pick it up when boarding. Most shops refuse to take any orders less than half an hour before the take-off of your flight.

A East Side Airlines Terminal, First Avenue and 37th Street; tel. 697-3374

JFK Express information, tel. 858-7272 (9 a.m. to midnight)

B **BABY-SITTERS*.** You should be able to obtain the names of baby-sitting agencies from the hotel receptionist, or consult the Yellow Pages of the telephone directory. The Baby Sitters Guild can usually send someone over on short notice. Call morning or afternoon for an evening booking. There is a minimum number of hours, and you pay the sitter's car fare.

Baby Sitters Guild, 60 East 42nd Street (tel. 682-0227)

BICYCLE RENTAL*. Taking a spin in Central Park—closed to cars on Sundays and certain other days—is a great change of pace from city life. A list of rental agencies can be found in the Yellow Pages of the telephone directory under "Bicycles—Dealers and Rental". You can rent by the half-day or more. A refundable deposit is required.

Information on cycle tours is given in a book by R. Macia, *The N.Y. Bicycler,* and by American Youth Hostels (see ACCOMMODATION) and a cyclers' association called The Transportation Alternative:

2121 Broadway, New York, NY 10023 (tel. 799-6024)

BOAT EXCURSIONS. Splendid views of the city are in store when you take one of a variety of boat trips around Manhattan.

The Circle Line leaves from Pier 83 at the foot of West 43rd Street for a three-hour cruise around Manhattan. You can take a ferry from Battery Park to Ellis Island, where there is a guided tour by the National Park Service Rangers or to the Statue of Liberty. The Staten Island Ferry also leaves from Battery Park and offers an impressive view of Manhattan and the Statue of Liberty, even if you don't have time to get off and visit Staten Island itself.

For something further afield, cruise up the Hudson River to West Point, an all-day affair; departure from Pier 81 at the foot of West 41st Street.

Circle Line, tel. 563-3200

Ellis Island and Statue of Liberty ferries, tel. 269-5755

Staten Island ferry, tel. 806-6940

Hudson River Day Line, tel. 279-5151

CAMPING. Although there are no campsites in New York City itself, you'll find a few on Long Island (such as Hither Hills at Montauk) and in the Hudson River Valley. Most open in May and close in September or October. Remember to make advance reservations if it's for July or August.

A comprehensive booklet on camping in New York State can be obtained from the New York Department of Commerce, Division of Tourism:

99 Washington Avenue, Albany, NY 12245

Within New York State, call 1-800-342-3810 (no charge); if phoning from another state, dial 1-518-474-4116 (toll call).

You can get maps and information on backpacking and camping in the Adirondack and Catskill Forest Preserves from the Bureau of Forest Recreation, New York State Department of Environmental Conservation:

50 Wolf Road, Albany, NY 12233

CAR RENTAL and DRIVING

Rental. Cars can be hired at the airports or in New York City from one of many rental agencies (listed in the Yellow Pages under "Automobile Renting & Leasing"). Prices are competitive, and you can save a substantial amount of money if you shop around. If you want to be sure of obtaining a particular model at the airport, however, make arrangements through an international agency before leaving home. Some rental firms give 10% discounts to foreign visitors, others propose special weekend and unlimited-mileage rates or rent-it-here, leave-it-there deals.

In summer, ask for an air-conditioned car, which costs nothing extra. If you want to hire one of the less expensive models, you should give the company at least one week's notice. Whatever the model, it's a good idea to reserve a week in advance for weekend rentals from mid-May to mid-September.

Unless you pay by major credit card, you'll have to make a large cash deposit. You must be at least 21 (18 when paying by credit card) and have a valid driving licence and passport.

If you'd like to cross the country cheaply, look into an auto-drive-away deal. If you have references in America and you meet certain conditions, you may be engaged to drive someone else's car to a specified destination. A refundable security deposit is required, then the

C car is turned over to you with one tank of petrol. The driver pays all other expenses. For further information, contact Autodrive-away Co.:
42 Broadway Downtown, suite 1827, New York, NY 10004
(tel. 221-6930)

Driving conditions. Although New York City is best avoided by car, you may wish to explore Long Island, Connecticut or other surrounding areas. If you *must* drive a car in New York City, remember certain rules: the speed limit is 30 miles per hour unless otherwise indicated; you may not use your horn in town; and, of course, visitors from the U.K. must remember to drive on the right. Be sure you are fully insured; if you are responsible for an accident, fines can be high.

Parking. The city operates several municipal parking lots. It's a good idea to use them, since it's next to impossible to find a parking place on the street. If you do happen to find one, obey posted parking regulations. Never park next to a fire hydrant and don't leave your car on the street over the time limit, or it may be towed away—a costly proposition!

Highways (motorways) and bridges. There are several terms used for different types of highways, and most of these (except for expressways) collect tolls. Toll highways may be called "thruways", "parkways" (usually lined with shrubs, flowers or trees) or "turnpikes". You should keep a stock of change for convenience when travelling; most toll areas have baskets for drivers with correct change; you simply drop in the right amount so there's no waiting. The speed limit on all superhighways is 55 m.p.h. Limits are strictly enforced.
   In New York, there are 65 bridges; tolls of varying amounts must be paid on almost all of them.

Petrol. Service stations are few and far between in the city. They are usually closed in the evening and on Sundays.

Breakdowns and insurance. The Automobile Club of New York (ACNY), a branch of the American Automobile Association (AAA), will help members, as well as foreign visitors affiliated with other recognized automobile associations. In case of breakdown or for other problems along the way, call their highway service at 695-8311; or wait until a state police patrol car comes along.

In New York City, the ACNY is located at:

108 28 East 78th Street (tel. 586-1166)

The AAA also offers information on travelling in the U.S., as well as short-term insurance for visitors (1–12 months).

AAA World Wide Travel, 8111 Gatehouse Road, Falls Church, VA 22047

Road signs. You will encounter some international road signs, but you may see the following written signs as well:

American	*British*
Detour	Deviation
Divided highway	Dual carriageway
Expressway	Motorway
Men working	Roadworks
No passing	No overtaking
No parking along highway	Clearway
Railroad crossing	Level crossing
Roadway	Carriageway
Traffic circle	Roundabout
Yield	Give way

CIGARETTES, CIGARS, TOBACCO*. Cigarettes vary in price depending on where you buy them. A packet from a vending machine always costs much more than one obtained in a supermarket or at a newsstand. Cigarettes are cheaper when bought by the carton. British-made brands can be twice as expensive as local ones.

The choice of pipe tobacco, both home-grown and imported, is vast, and New Yorkers even claim that their city is the world's cigar capital (though you won't find any from Cuba; they're not available in the U.S.).

CLOTHING. In New York you have to cope with extremes of temperature, not just between winter and summer, but even between outdoors and indoors. Despite the energy crisis, some Americans still persist in overheating in winter and overcooling in summer.

In winter, a heavy coat is a necessity. Under it wear several layers of lighter clothes, which can be shed according to the temperature indoors. Don't forget your winter boots, warm hat and gloves. Only Canadians could call New York winters mild.

In summer wear your lightest clothes, in natural fibres if possible. The air is so humid and sticky that you'll need several changes of clothing. Carry a sweater to ward off the chill you'll feel indoors in the frigid New York air conditioning. Bring along a raincoat, too, for you

C may well be caught in a downpour. Rubber overshoes are very practical and sold in any department store.

Americans are known for wearing casual clothes; however there are still some bars and restaurants that stipulate jacket and tie, particularly in the evening.

COMMUNICATIONS

Post offices. The U.S. Post Office, unlike its British counterpart, deals only with mail. Branches are generally open from 9 a.m. to 5 p.m. Monday to Friday, from 9 a.m. to 12 noon on Saturdays. New York's General Post Office (see below) keeps longer hours, from 7.30 a.m. to 6 p.m. Monday to Saturday. Self-service facilities in the lobby are always available.

You can buy stamps at the reception desk in your hotel or from stamp machines (often found in public buildings or stores where stationery is sold). Stamps sold by machine cost more than at the post office.

You'll find the standard blue mailboxes on almost every street.

Mail. If you don't know where you'll be staying in New York, you can have mail sent to you c/o General Delivery (poste restante) to the General Post Office:

380 West 33rd Street, New York, NY 10001

American Express will also accept mail for foreign visitors (without charge if you hold their credit card or traveller's cheques); envelopes should be marked "Client's Mail".

The mail should be collected within 30 days. Take your passport along for identification.

Telegrams and telex. American telegraph companies are privately run. The main companies, such as RCA and Western Union (Western Union International for overseas), are listed in the Yellow Pages directory under "Telegraph". You can telephone the telegraph office, dictate the message and have the charge added to your hotel bill, or dictate it from a coin-operated phone and pay on the spot. A letter telegram (night letter) costs about half the rate of a normal telegram but takes at least twice as long to arrive.

Telex services are offered by the same companies.

Telephone. Public telephones can be found in hotel lobbies, restaurants, drugstores, rail and air terminals, gas stations, sidewalk booths **110** and along the highway. Directions for use are on the instrument.

Telephone rates are listed and explained in the front of the White Pages of the telephone directory. Also included is information on person-to-person (personal) calls, collect (reverse-charge) calls, conference, station-to-station and credit-card calls. All numbers with an 800 prefix are toll-free (no charge). There are reductions for phoning at night, on weekends and on holidays.

Long-distance call charges are calculated per minute; direct-dialling is the easiest and fastest method even from a phone booth. After three minutes the operator will interrupt to tell you to add more money. If you need assistance, dial "0" and ask for an overseas operator.

Some useful numbers:

Big Apple Report (news, theatre, traffic)	976-2323
Parks (special events, usually free)	755-4100
Time	976-1616
Weather	976-1212

COMPLAINTS. If you feel you have reason to complain about retail stores or business practices, you should contact New York City Department of Consumer Affairs:

80 Lafayette Street, New York, NY 10013 (tel. 577-0111)

For complaints about taxi drivers or taxi fares, see under TRANSPORT.

CONSULATES. If you plan to stay in the United States for more than a month you should register with your consulate. This will facilitate things in case you lose your passport, for example.

Australia	636 Fifth Avenue; tel. 245-4000
Canada	1251 Avenue of the Americas; tel. 586-2400
Eire	580 Fifth Avenue; tel. 382-2525
New Zealand	Suite 530, 630 Fifth Avenue; tel. 586-0060
South Africa	425 Park Avenue; tel. 838-1700
United Kingdom	845 Third Avenue; tel. 752-8400

CRIME and THEFT. It's true that New York City's crime rate is high, that theft is common, and tourists are always easy targets for robbery. By taking a few simple precautions, you can reduce the risk:

● always lock your hotel room door
● deposit valuables in the hotel safe

- never carry large amounts of cash on you, and always wear a minimum of jewellery (watches, chains and even shoulder bags can be all too easily torn off)
- carry as much of your money as possible in the form of traveller's cheques, and keep a record of these (and your passport) separate from the cheques themselves
- avoid side streets or obviously seedy areas
- never leave valuables (bags, etc.) unattended or behind your back (at airports, railway stations, restaurants, on beaches, etc.) even for a few seconds

And if you *are,* in fact, robbed, don't play the hero; hand over what you have. Then report it to the police immediately (tel. 374-5000, 911 for emergencies): your insurance company will need to see a copy of the police report (as will your consulate if your passport is stolen). As for stolen or lost traveller's cheques, report the matter at once to the bank that issued them so that payment can be stopped immediately.

CUSTOMS and ENTRY REGULATIONS. See also AIRPORTS. To enter the United States, foreign visitors need a valid passport and a visitor's visa, which can be obtained at any U.S. embassy or consulate. Canadians need only present proof of nationality. Everyone must fill out customs declaration forms before arrival (usually distributed by your airline near the end of the flight).

The following chart shows certain duty-free items you may take into the U.S. (if you are over 21) and, when returning home, into your own country:

Into:	Cigarettes	Cigars		Tobacco	Spirits		Wine
U.S.A.	200	or 50	or	1,350 g.	1 l.	or	1 l.
Australia	200	or 250 g. or		250 g.	1 l.	or	1 l.
Canada	200	and 50	and	900 g.	1.1 l.	or	1.1 l.
Eire	200	or 50	or	250 g.	1 l.	and	2 l.
N. Zealand	200	or 50	or	½ lb.	1 qt.	and	1 qt.
S. Africa	400	and 50	and	250 g.	1 l.	and	1 l.
U.K.	200	or 50	or	250 g.	1 l.	and	2 l.

A non-resident may claim, free of duty and taxes, articles up to $100 in value for use as gifts for other persons. The exemption is valid only if the gifts accompany you, if you stay 72 hours or more and have not claimed this exemption within the preceding 6 months. Up to 100 cigars may be included within this gift exemption.

Plants and foodstuffs also are subject to strict control; visitors from abroad may not import fruits, vegetables or meat. The same goes for chocolates that contain liqueur.

Arriving and departing passengers should report any money or cheques, etc., exceeding a total of $5,000.

DRUGS. The possession of any drugs—be it soft or hard—is usually considered a jailable offense. For a foreigner, it may mean expulsion from the U.S., and expulsion for life, without mentioning the possibility of horrendous fines.

ELECTRIC CURRENT. 110–115-volt 60-cycle A.C. is standard throughout the U.S. Plugs are the flat, two-pronged variety. Visitors from abroad will need a transformer (240–110 V) and probably an adaptor plug for their electric razors.

EMERGENCIES

All-purpose emergency number:	911
Doctors' Emergency Service (not for hospitalization):	745-5900
Dentists' Emergency Service: 679-4172, after 8 p.m.:	679-3966

The telephone operator can also connect you with emergency services, dial "0".

GUIDES*. Several agencies offer organized tours and special excursions (helicopter, night-club rounds, historical tours, etc.). Individual sightseeing guides are also available. For details, contact the New York Convention & Visitors Bureau:

2 Columbus Circle, New York, NY 10019; tel. 397-8222

HAIRDRESSERS and BARBERS*. There are plenty of barbers, and women's hairdressers usually accept male customers as well. During the week you can be fitted in fairly promptly in most establishments, but you should book ahead for a Saturday appointment.

C

D

E

G

H

L **LANGUAGE.** You may take time adjusting to the New York accent if you come from London, Sydney or Glasgow. But don't be discouraged—even Americans from Houston or San Francisco have the same problem.

Certain words have different meanings for Americans and British. Here are a few which could be a source of confusion:

U.S.	British	U.S.	British
admission	entry fee	pavement	road surface
bathroom	toilet (private)	purse/pocket-	handbag
bill	note (money)	book	
billfold	wallet	rest room	toilet (public)
check	bill	round-trip	return
	(restaurant)	(ticket)	
collect call	reverse charges	second floor	first floor
elevator	lift	sidewalk	pavement
first floor	ground floor	stand in line	queue up
gasoline	petrol	subway	underground
liquor	spirits	trailer	caravan
liquor store	off-licence	underpass	subway

LAUNDRY and DRY-CLEANING. Your hotel may have efficient same-day service and some even provide drying lines in the bathroom.

You can also find self-service laundries where coin-operated washing-machines and dryers are available. Look under "Laundries—self service" in the Manhattan Yellow Pages or ask your hotel receptionist.

Dry-cleaners usually provide one-day service. They are also listed in the telephone directory's Yellow Pages under "Cleaners and Dryers". Self-service dry-cleaners, where you pay according to weight, are well-run; each load takes about an hour.

LIQUOR REGULATIONS. Most alcoholic beverages are sold exclusively in licensed liquor stores. Only beer can be bought in supermarkets and grocery stores. Small restaurants that don't have the expensive permit to serve liquor will usually let you bring your own bottle of wine.

Most liquor stores are open until 9 or 10 p.m., sometimes even until midnight. They are not open on Sunday (beer is sold on Sunday after 12 noon). Another carry-over from Prohibition is the law that bottles (or beer cans) must be concealed when drinking in public. The minimum age for drinking any alcoholic beverage is 18.

LOST PROPERTY. Each transport system maintains its own lost-property office. It's reassuring to know that even in New York, dozens of items are turned in daily, sometimes valuable ones.

New York City Transit Lost Property (subway network and
Brooklin, Queens, Staten Island bus system)   tel. 625-6200

Taxi and Limousine Lost and Found   tel. 382-9309

MAPS. At the New York Convention & Visitors Bureau tourists can get a free map of Manhattan. Public transport route maps are available from bus drivers and at the toll booth in subway stations. Falk, who furnished the maps for this book, also publishes a complete series of detailed New York area maps.

MEDICAL CARE. See also EMERGENCIES. It's important for visitors from Britain to remember that the U.S. government does not provide free health services. Arrangements for temporary health and accident insurance should be made beforehand through your travel agency or an insurance company, or ask at your local Social Security office for precise information on coverage during your trip to the States. Tourists can purchase additional short-term insurance for journeys within the U.S. at the insurance counters and from the vending machines to be found everywhere in air, bus and rail terminals.

Except in an emergency, foreign visitors should call their consulate for a list of doctors in New York City. In any emergency, medical or otherwise, local telephone operators are an excellent source of advice.

Drugstores. A prescription is required for most medicines. There are numerous drugstores, but only one is open day and night, seven days a week:

Kaufman, Lexington Avenue at 50th Street (tel. 755-2266)

MEETING PEOPLE. Central Park on Sunday is the place to do it—or one of the countless "mixer" bars and other night spots. Don't be surprised if strangers in elevators start up a conversation, as Americans tend to be outgoing.

Like city dwellers everywhere, New Yorkers are often tense and in a hurry. In a restaurant or post office, your "Thank you" may only meet with a grunt in reply. It's quite usual and means "Not at all". Even Americans from outside the city are amazed at the self-absorption of New Yorkers. The only answer to your questions in the street may be a shrug. However, at gatherings (such as parties) New Yorkers show themselves to be friendly and interested in meeting people.

MONEY MATTERS

Currency. The dollar is divided into 100 cents.

Coins: 1¢ (penny), 5¢ (nickel), 10¢ (dime), 25¢ (quarter), 50¢ (half dollar) and $1.

Banknotes: $1, $2 (rare), $5, $10, $20, $50 and $100. Larger denominations ($500 and $1,000) are not in general circulation. All denominations are the same size and same green colour, so be sure to double-check your cash before you spend it.

For currency restrictions, see CUSTOMS AND ENTRY REGULATIONS.

Banks and currency exchange. Most banks are open from 9 a.m. to 3 p.m. Monday to Friday.

If you arrive on the weekend, be sure to change some money before leaving the airport, where currency exchange offices remain open. You may be able to change money at your hotel, though you probably won't get the bank rate. Note that banks usually prefer to change only small sums of foreign money.

N.B. Visitors from abroad should bear in mind that foreign money cannot be changed in most banks; you have to go to certain ones, like Citibank. Therefore it's best to carry dollars with you, in cash or traveller's cheques.

Make sure you always have a supply of $1 banknotes (for taxis, toll bridges, tipping, etc.)—they are invariably useful.

Deak-Perera, which changes foreign currency and cashes American and foreign traveller's cheques, has a midtown office at:

630 Fifth Avenue (between 50th and 51st streets)

Credit cards. Credit cards play a far greater role here than in Europe. In the U.S., they are a way of life, and most Americans have several. The major cards are accepted as cash almost everywhere. When paying for goods or services, including hotel and restaurant bills, you will be asked: "Cash or charge?", meaning you have the choice of paying either in cash or in "plastic money". You'll need to show two pieces of identification when charging a purchase.

Traveller's cheques. Visitors from abroad will find traveller's cheques drawn on American banks far easier to deal with. Only cash small
amounts at a time, and keep the balance of your cheques in the hotel

safe if possible. At the very least, be sure to keep your receipt and a list of the serial numbers of the cheques in a separate place to facilitate a refund in case of loss or theft.

Sales tax. Expect to have state and city taxes, a total of 8%, added to the marked-up price of all goods purchased in New York City, including meals, clothing and hotel accommodation.

NEWSPAPERS and MAGAZINES. The city's major newspapers are the *Daily News,* the *New York Times* and the *New York Post. The Sunday Times* includes a particularly comprehensive arts and leisure section, useful for visitors. The weekly publications—*The New Yorker, New York* and *The Village Voice*—are helpful for finding out what's going on in theatres, nightclubs, museums, art galleries, concert halls and in the world of sports.

For the best selection of foreign newspapers and magazines, go to Hotalings at 142 West 42nd Street or the news-stands on the south side of West 42nd Street between Avenue of the Americas and Fifth Avenue.

PHOTOGRAPHY. All popular brands of film and photographic equipment are available. Try to buy in discount stores where prices are much lower. Black-and-white and colour film usually take at least a week to be developed, colour slides about two weeks.

Some airport security machines use X-rays which can ruin your film. Ask that it be checked separately, or enclose it in a lead-lined bag.

You can also buy film and equipment at the Kodak Film Center. Experts there will be happy to answer any questions you may have about taking pictures. It's situated at

60 East 42nd Street (tel. 490-9130)

The staff at Nikon House will gladly advise you about equipment. While you're there, you may want to have a look at the current exhibition of photography, on view in the gallery at

620 Fifth Avenue (tel. 586-3907)

Amateurs and professionals alike will want to visit the International Center of Photography, a museum dedicated to the photographic arts, at

Fifth Avenue and 94th Street (tel. 860-1777)

P **POLICE.** For information or assistance don't hesitate to stop a policeman on the street. You'll find him courteous and ready to help. New York police are easy to recognize with their blue uniforms, flat caps and bulging jackets. Their bulky equipment includes a gun, nightstick, handcuffs and walkie-talkie. They often travel in pairs. Some mounted policemen patrol the parks.

In case of emergency call 911 (police, ambulance, fire). See also the section CRIME AND THEFT.

PUBLIC HOLIDAYS. Banks and most stores are closed on the following Monday if certain holidays (e.g. Christmas) are on Sunday. They close on Friday if those holidays fall on Saturday.

New Year's Day	January 1
Lincoln's Birthday*	February 12
Washington's Birthday	Third Monday in February
Memorial Day	Last Monday in May
Independence Day	July 4
Labor Day	First Monday in September
Columbus Day	Second Monday in October
Veterans' Day	November 11
Thanksgiving	Fourth Thursday in November
Christmas Day	December 25

R **RADIO and TV.** You'll almost certainly have radio and television in your hotel room, with a vast choice of programmes.

It's difficult to choose among all the radio programmes. In New York there are about 60 AM-FM stations.

Television stations broadcast from 6 a.m. until around 3 or 4 the next morning. The main networks are on channels 2, 4 and 7. Channel 13, the educational network, has no commercials. The major news broadcasts come at 7 a.m. and 7 p.m. Most programmes are in colour.

There's an interesting Museum of Broadcasting at
1 East 53rd Street (tel. 752-7684)

Call before going for a recorded message of special events scheduled for the week.

_____
* Not celebrated nationwide.

RELIGIOUS SERVICES. Every conceivable religion is represented in New York; not only the well-known faiths but a large number of off-beat sects also hold services.

Over 40 churches of special interest are mentioned in the free "Visitor's Guide and Map" issued by the N.Y. Convention & Visitors Bureau (see TOURIST INFORMATION OFFICES). A list of the main churches is posted in most hotel lobbies.

Here's a cross-section for different beliefs:

Catholic: St. Patrick's Cathedral, Fifth Avenue (opposite Rockefeller Center), tel. 753-2261

Episcopalian: Cathedral of St. John the Divine (the largest Gothic-style church in the world), Amsterdam Avenue and 112th Street, tel. 678-6888

Jewish: Temple Emanu-El, Fifth Avenue at 65th Street, tel. 744-1400

Methodist: Lexington United Methodist Church, 150 East 62nd Street, tel. 838-6915

Moslem: Islamic Center, Riverside Drive and 72nd Street, tel. 362-6800

Presbyterian: Central Presbyterian, 593 Park Avenue, tel. 838-0808

Zen Studies Society: 223 East 67th Street, tel. 861-3333

SIGHTSEEING HOURS. To save you a futile trip, here is a list of New York's leading museums and attractions with their opening hours. A prior check is never wasted, however, as changes do inevitably occur.

American Museum of Immigration, see Statue of Liberty ferry on p. 120.

American Museum of Natural History: 10 a.m.–5.45 p.m. Mon., Tues., Thurs., Sun., till 9 p.m. Wed., Fri., Sat.

Bronx Zoo: 10 a.m.–5 p.m. daily (till 5.30 p.m. Sun.).

Brooklyn Museum: 10 a.m.–5 p.m. Wed.–Sat., noon–5 p.m. Sun.

Castle Clinton: Talks by park rangers 11 a.m.–3 p.m. Open 9 a.m.–5 p.m. Mon.–Fri.

City Hall: 10 a.m.–3.30 p.m. Mon.–Fri.

Cloisters: 10 a.m.–4.45 p.m. Tues.–Sat., 1–4.45 p.m. Sun.

Cooper-Hewitt Museum: 10 a.m.–9 p.m. Tues., 10 a.m.–5 p.m. Wed.–Sat., noon–5 p.m. Sun.

S **Federal Hall National Memorial:** 9 a.m.–5 p.m. daily (closed on weekends in winter).

Fraunces Tavern Museum: 10 a.m.–4 p.m. Mon.–Fri.

Frick Collection: 10 a.m.–6 p.m. Tues.–Sat., 1–6 p.m. Sun. (June, July, August also closed Tues.).

Guggenheim Museum: 11 a.m.–8 p.m. Tues., 11 a.m.–5 p.m. Wed.–Sun.

International Center of Photography: noon–8 p.m. Tues.–Fri., noon–6 p.m. Sat., Sun.

Jewish Museum: noon–5 p.m. Mon.–Thurs., 11 a.m.–6. p.m. Sun.

Lincoln Center: Guided tours from 10.30 a.m. to 5 p.m. daily.

Metropolitan Museum of Art: 10 a.m.–8.45 p.m. Tues., 10 a.m.–4.45 p.m. Wed.–Sat., 11 a.m.–4.45 p.m. Sun.

Morris-Jumel Mansion: 10 a.m.–4 p.m. Tues.–Sun.

Museum of American Folk Art: 10.30 a.m.–5.30 p.m. Wed.–Sun. (till 8 p.m. Tues.).

Museum of the American Indian: 10 a.m.–5 p.m. Tues.–Sat., 1–5 p.m. Sun.

Museum of the City of New York: 10 a.m.–5 p.m. Tues.–Sat., 1–5 p.m. Sun.

Museum of Holography: noon–6 p.m. Wed.–Sun. (till 9 p.m. Thurs.).

Museum of Modern Art: 11 a.m.–6 p.m. Fri.–Tues., 11 a.m.–9 p.m. Thurs., closed Wed.

New York Botanical Garden Conservatory: 10 a.m.–4 p.m. Tues.–Sun.

New York Experience: Hourly shows from 11 a.m. Mon.–Sat., from noon Sun.

New-York Historical Society: 11 a.m.–5 p.m. Tues.–Fri., 10 a.m.–5 p.m. Sat., 1–5 p.m. Sun.

Pierpont Morgan Library: 10.30 a.m.–5 p.m. Tues.–Sat., 1–5 p.m. Sun.

Rockefeller Center: Guided tours from 9.45 a.m. to 4.45 p.m. Mon.–Sat. Observation Roof: Oct.–March, 10.30 a.m.–7 p.m. Mon.–Sun.; April–Sept., 10 a.m.–9 p.m. Mon.–Sun.

South Street Seaport Museum: 11 a.m.–6 p.m. daily.

Statue of Liberty ferry: Hourly from 9 a.m. to 4 p.m. every day.

Stock Exchange: 9.45 a.m.–4 p.m. Mon.–Fri.

United Nations: Guided tours every day at 20-minute intervals from 9 a.m. to 4.45 p.m.

Whitney Museum of American Art: 11 a.m.–8 p.m. Tues., 11 a.m.–6 p.m. Wed.–Sat., noon–6 p.m. Sun.

World Trade Center, Observation Deck: 9.30 a.m.–9.30 p.m. daily.

THEATRE and CONCERT TICKETS. Seats for new or nearly new Broadway shows can be very difficult to obtain, particularly for the musicals. Ask at your hotel desk: the receptionist may be able to get you tickets for a small commission. There are countless ticket agencies in the Broadway/Times Square neighbourhood, or you can try at the "Ticketron" counters in Grand Central Station, Madison Square Garden or Macy's (they handle rock concerts, sports and other events, too), or at the theatre box office itself.

"TKTS" (Times Square Theater Center), at Broadway and 47th Street, is a non-profit organization that sells tickets on the day of the performance at slightly over half price. They are open from noon till 2 p.m. for matinées, and from 3 till 8 p.m. for evening performances. Get there early, as the waiting line may be quite long; but the savings are well worth the wait. The "TKTS" booth in 2 World Trade Center handles tickets for evening shows only (11.30 a.m.–5.30 p.m. Mon.–Fri., 11 a.m.–3 p.m. Sat.). Lines here are shorter.

Holders of major credit cards can book tickets by phoning "Tele-Charge" (tel. 239-6200) or "Chargit" (tel. 944-9300). Tickets can then be picked up at the theatre on presentation of the credit card.

The Bryant Park Ticket Booth (Bryant Park side of 42nd Street, between 5th and 6th) sells half-price tickets for concerts and dance performances the same day. Payment must be made in cash or traveller's cheques. The booth opens daily from noon to 7 p.m.

TIMES and DATES. The continental United States has a total of four time zones; New York City is on Eastern Standard Time. In summer (between April and October) Daylight Saving Time is adopted and clocks move ahead one hour. The following chart shows the time in various cities in winter when it's noon in New York City:

Los Angeles	**New York**	London	Sydney
9 a.m. Sunday	**noon** **Sunday**	5 p.m. Sunday	4 a.m. Monday

For the exact time in New York, call 976-1616.

Dates in the U.S. are written differently from those in Great Britain; for example: 1/6/99 means January 6, 1999.

T **TIPPING.** Service is never included in restaurant bills. The usual tip is 15–20% (an easy way to work it out is to double the 8% tax marked on your bill). Cinema or theatre ushers and filling-station attendants are not tipped. See the chart below for further guidelines.

Porter, per bag	50¢ –$1 (minimum $1)
Hotel maid (not for overnight stay)	$1 per day or $5 per week
Guide	10–15%
Lavatory attendant	50¢
Taxi driver	15–20%
Hairdresser/Barber	15–20%

TOILETS. You can find toilets in restaurants, museums, railway stations and large stores. In some places you must deposit a dime, in others you should leave a tip for the attendant.

Americans use the terms "rest room", "powder room", "bathroom" (private) and "ladies'" or "men's room" to indicate the toilet.

TOURIST INFORMATION OFFICES. *New York Convention & Visitors Bureau* is a non-profit organization subsidized by the city's hotels and merchants. The staff will give you city maps and leaflets about principal tourist attractions, a price list of major hotels and any further information you may require:

2 Columbus Circle; tel. 397-8222. Hours: 9 a.m.–6 p.m., daily

An information booth at Broadway and 42nd Street gives out pamphlets.

Traveler's Aid Society dispenses just about everything, even—for the traveller in distress who looks a serious enough proposition—pocket money. In New York City, it's located at:

204 East 39th Street (tel. 679-0200)

The *Automobile Club of New York* (ACNY) offers helpful advice on motoring in the U.S. If you plan to spend more than 60 days in the United States, you can obtain a regular membership for a modest fee which includes free services such as emergency road service, complete towing service and all AAA touring publications necessary for your trip. They also give information on how to get to your destination by car or public transport. Call 594-0700.

ACNY International Travel Department, 28 East 78th Street; tel. 586-1166

For information prior to arrival in the U.S., contact:

United States Travel Service, 22 Sackville Street, London W1; tel. (01) 439 74 33

TRANSPORT

Buses*. New York City buses are convenient for travelling crosstown (east and west), especially since the subway system runs essentially north and south. There are buses on every avenue, too, except upper Park Avenue. They cost the same as the subway, and tokens can be used. You must have the right change to deposit in the box beside the driver. Children under six travel free.

When travelling north or south, always ask first to make sure the bus goes to your destination. Otherwise you may find yourself in Queens when you thought you were heading for the upper East Side.

Inter-city coach service. Buses will take you virtually anywhere in the country. The two largest coach companies, Greyhound Lines and Continental Trailways leave from the Port Authority Bus Terminal (Eighth Avenue and 41st Street) in Manhattan, one block west of Times Square.

Tourists can buy "unlimited travel tickets" (these can also be purchased outside the U.S.) good for a given length of time, to go anywhere in the country by bus at a flat rate.

Greyhound Lines, tel. 635-0800, Continental Trailways, tel. 730-7460

Subway*. This comprehensive underground network is the fastest means of transport in New York. Trains run 24 hours a day. Maps of the network are posted in every station and train. The subway is safe, generally speaking, in daytime. At night, while there are real dangers, don't exaggerate them. It is however, certainly wiser to take a taxi at night if you can. A few tips on safety:

● in late evening or at night, take a carriage in the middle, the one in which the conductor is riding

● never wait on the edge of the platform, keep to the middle

● if the platform is empty, do not wait there but beside the token-purchase booth

T It's not easy to use the subway: you'll need two or three days to master the subtleties of the system. Don't hesitate to ask a passerby or a policeman for help. Look carefully before you enter to be sure you're going in the right direction: "Downtown" means south and street numbers are lower; "Uptown" is north, with higher street numbers. Most subway lines run north-south; to go "crosstown", take the shuttle train from Times Square to Grand Central.

The first car always shows the name or number of the train and the terminus. The New York subway system has three lines—the IRT, BMT and IND—each with its own track networks. Transfers can be made between lines at certain points. Local trains use the outside tracks, express trains the centre ones. You'll soon get used to the abbreviations, such as "B'way" for Broadway.

To take the subway, you need a token (purchased at the booth in any station) which you insert in the turnstile; this entitles you to ride as far as you like. Buy a handful of tokens at a time; they're also good for buses. Subway maps, when available, can be obtained free at the booth. See also map on p. 53.

Taxis*. There are around 12,000 taxis in New York, all bright yellow. Just stand on a street corner for a minute or two and hail one driving by. When the word "Taxi" is illuminated, the cab is free. An "Off Duty" sign indicates the taxi is not available.

Fares are clearly marked in black on the door. A small surcharge is made at night (8 p.m.–6 a.m.) and on Sundays, though it doesn't show up on the meter. The driver is entitled to charge extra for baggage, but most don't bother. If your route comprises a toll tunnel or bridge, you must pay the toll.

Should you have a complaint to make about a driver, note his name and number and contact the N.Y. Taxi Commission:

tel. 382-9301

Avoid taxis without a medallion no matter what discount they may offer – these unauthorized cabs are not reliable.

If you're nervous about getting to the airport on time, on a wet day for example, you can book a cab through:

UTOG Taxi Radio, tel. 741-2000
Skyline Radio Taxi, tel. 741-1800

Taxi drivers have no obligation to change banknotes of denominations higher than $5 (it's more than wise to have with you at all times some $1 banknotes—they constantly come in handy). You should give the driver a tip of at least 15%, more for special service.

Trains. Development of America's railroads has followed a zig-zag path between neglect and renewed interest, leaving them in a state something less than top-notch, but, on the East Coast, the service is adequate, sometimes very good. Reserving a seat can be a gamble, however. You may be lucky enough to pick an ultramodern car complete with bar and air-conditioning, or you might end up in a dilapidated coach dating from another era.

Amtrak (National Railroad Passenger Corporation) offers U.S.A. Rail-passes (flat-rate unlimited rail travel for a given period of time). Various package deals are also available through Amtrak for link-ups with car rental agencies, bus companies and hotel groups—even so-called "railsail" packages, connecting with Caribbean cruises.

If you're going to one of the large cities on the eastern seaboard (Boston, Philadelphia, Washington) or to Montreal, take the "Metroliner", a luxury train belonging to Amtrak. It costs a bit more, but you get there faster and in comfort. You can book seats in advance by phone and pick up your tickets at the counter when you arrive (tel. 736-4545).

In New York City there are three main stations: **Penn** (Pennsylvania) **Station,** underneath Madison Square Garden at 34th Street and Eighth Avenue, is the most important for long-distance travel and also serves Long Island commuters. **Grand Central Station,** on 42nd Street between Park and Lexington avenues, has both suburban and long-distance lines. **PATH Station,** for trains to New Jersey, is located below the World Trade Center.

WATER. New York water is perfectly safe to drink. Due to periodic water shortages, you'll only be given a glass of water in a restaurant if you ask for one. Club soda (fizzy water) is used mostly in cocktails. Uncarbonated (flat) mineral water can be bought in a grocery store.

WEIGHTS and MEASURES. The United States is one of the last countries in the world to change to the metric system and is not yet involved in an official changeover programme. Some British visitors will be happy to go back to the good old days of feet and inches.

Milk and fruit juice can be bought by the quart or half-gallon, but wine and spirits now come in litre bottles. Food products usually have the weight marked in ounces and pounds as well as in grammes.

There are some slight differences between British and American measures, for instance:

1 U.S. gallon = .833 British Imp. gallon = 3.8 litres
1 U.S. quart = .833 British Imp. quart = .9 litres

Index

An asterisk (*) next to a page number indicates a map reference. For index to Practical Information, see also p. 103.

128